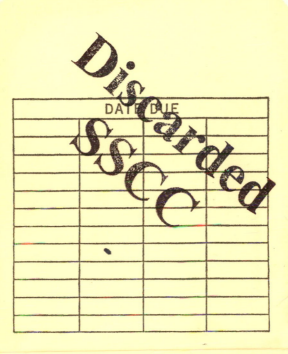

Pierre Boulle

Twayne's World Authors Series
French Literature

David O'Connell, Editor
Georgia State University

TWAS 859

PIERRE BOULLE.
Photograph courtesy Julliard.

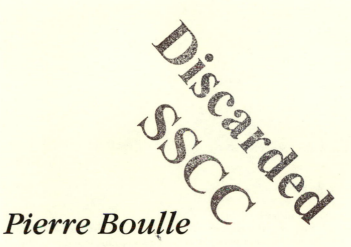

Pierre Boulle

Lucille Frackman Becker

Drew University

Twayne Publishers
An Imprint of Simon & Schuster Macmillan
New York

Prentice Hall International
London Mexico City New Delhi Singapore Sydney Toronto

Twayne's World Authors Series No. 859

Pierre Boulle
Lucille Frackman Becker

Twayne Publishers
An Imprint of Simon & Schuster Macmillan
866 Third Avenue
New York, NY 10022

Library of Congress Cataloging-in-Publication Data

Becker, Lucille Frackman.
    Pierre Boulle / Lucille Frackman Becker.
        p.   cm. — (Twayne's world authors series ; TWAS 859)
    Includes bibliographical references and index.
    ISBN 0-8057-8272-9
    1. Boulle, Pierre, 1912–   —Criticism and interpretation.
    I. Title.   II. Series.
    PQ2603.0754Z57   1995
    843'.914—dc20   95-31746
                                                                            CIP

10 9 8 7 6 5 4 3 2 1

Printed in the United States of America

Contents

Preface

The most important element in a work of fiction, according to Pierre Boulle, is the story it tells. Without a plot, he maintains, there is neither a novel nor a short story. But the story alone, however fascinating it may be, is insufficient in and of itself to constitute an outstanding literary work; certain additional elements are required to raise it above mere narrative. It is these essential elements that I discuss throughout the volume as I detail the way in which Boulle transcends his outstanding gifts as a storyteller to create a superior oeuvre.

Drawing heavily from Boulle's work in an effort to present him as much as possible in his own words, I trace in chapter 1 in three autobiographical works the background of his literary production as well as the source of his major themes. The bildungsroman *L'îlon* describes Boulle's early years in his native Provence; the autobiographical novel *Le sacrilège malais* relates his experiences as a rubber planter in Malaya and provides the background and many of the themes of the novels and tales that take place in Southeast Asia; and the third, *Aux sources de la rivière Kwaï*, tells of his heroic wartime adventures, which are more incredible than any that occur in his novels. It is here that the background and atmosphere for his most famous novel *Le pont de la rivière Kwaï* can be found.

Chapter 2 is devoted to a study of variations on the dominant theme in Boulle's work, the human capacity for self-delusion. In a series of novels, as well as the historical work *L'étrange croisade de l'empéreur Frédéric II*, Boulle describes the transformation that takes place in a man under the pressure of events. The most remarkable version of this theme is found in *Le pont de la rivière Kwaï*, which is discussed in chapter 3 together with the other novels that take place in Southeast Asia. While Boulle's experiences as a planter and Resistance hero supplied the background and atmosphere for the works situated in Southeast Asia, his scientific education inspired the essay on cosmology *L'univers ondoyant* as well as a series of science fiction novels and short stories discussed in chapter 4, in particular the novel *La planète des singes*, a classic in the science fiction genre. Chapter 5 examines Boulle's short stories and philosophical tales, demonstrating the author's mastery of this genre, while his theories on the art of the novel and the role of the novelist are examined in chapter 6.

Throughout this work, I establish the unique position Boulle occupies in contemporary letters, as he answers to all of the reasons we read novels: to enjoy the fascination of a story, to enlarge our experience, to live vicariously, to be carried to faraway places, to gain new insights into the human condition.

Acknowledgment

I will always be grateful to Pierre Boulle for his kind and generous permission to quote from his letters, interviews, and works, as well as for his unfailing interest and courtesy. I am sorry that I was not able to complete this book—which expresses my admiration for both the man and his work—before his death, but this merely confirms his thesis that however good our intentions may be, there is always something that stands in the way of their realization. I shall miss him.

Acknowledgment

Chronology

1912 Pierre (François Marie-Louis) born in Avignon 20 February to Eugène, lawyer, and Thérèse (Seguin) Boulle.

1920 Family purchases country house, l'Ilon, on the banks of the Rhône River.

1927 Death of Eugène Boulle.

1930 Pierre Boulle completes secondary studies at lycée in Avignon and passes baccalauréat.

1931 *Licence ès sciences,* Sorbonne.

1933 *Diplôme d'ingénieur,* Ecole Supérieure d'Electricité.

1933–1935 Works as engineer in Clermont-Ferrand.

1936–1939 Holds position of rubber planter on Sungei Tinggi plantation in Malaya.

1939 Is mobilized as second lieutenant and posted to Indochina, November.

1940 Fall of France, June.

1940–1941 Holds various posts in Indochina—Cochin-China, Annam, Laos.

1941 Returns to Singapore and joins the Free French, August.

Receives commando training with English Force 136 where he learns the art of blowing up a bridge, fixing an explosive charge to the side of a ship, derailing a train, and killing an enemy sentry as silently as possible.

Japan attacks Pearl Harbor, Pacific Islands, Malaya, and the British possessions in China, 7 December. Free French decide to transfer their mission to Kunming, China.

1942 Makes last visit to plantations in Malaya and departs for Rangoon, Burma, under pseudonym P. J. Rule.

Leaves Rangoon 30 January and drives on Burma Road. Arrives in Kunming 4 February.

Departs from Kunming by mule train. Arrives at Pin-Ku-Yin, desolate mountain post.

Transfers to Muong-La, a Thai village on banks of the Nam-Na River, six miles from Indochinese border, May.

Descends the Nam-Na River on a raft to infiltrate Indochina, August. Captured by Thai villagers after five days and handed over to French authorities.

Is court-martialed, declared guilty of treason, reduced to the ranks, deprived of French nationality, and sentenced to hard labor for life, October.

1942–1944   Prison. Escape engineered October–November 1944 as a result of Allied victories.

1945   Repatriated to France. Awarded French Légion d'Honneur, Croix de Guerre, Médaille de la Résistance.

1945–1948   Returns to rubber plantation in Malaya.

1948   Leaves Malaya and returns to France to pursue career as writer. Sells all that he owns and moves into small hotel room in Paris to devote himself to writing.

1950   Publishes first novel *William Conrad.*

1951   Publishes autobiographical novel *Le sacrilège malais.*

1952   Publishes *Le pont de la rivière Kwaï.* Prix Sainte-Beuve for *Le pont de la rivière Kwaï.*

1953   Publishes collection of stories *Contes de l'absurde.* Grand Prix de la Nouvelle pour *Contes de l'absurde.* Publishes novel *La face.*

1954   Publishes novella *Le bourreau.*

1955   Moves into widowed sister's apartment in sixteenth arrondissement, where he helps to raise her young daughter and where he lives until his death.

Publishes novel *L'épreuve des hommes blancs.*

1957   Publishes collection of stories $E=mc^2$.

1958   Publishes novel *Les voies de salut* and screenplay *Walt Disney's Siam.*

1960 Publishes novel *Un métier de seigneur.*

1962 Publishes play *William Conrad.*

1963 Publishes novel *La planète des singes.*

1964 Publishes novel *Le jardin de Kanashima* and story collection *Histoires charitables.*

1966 Publishes autobiographical work *Aux sources de la rivière Kwaï.*

1967 Publishes novel *Le photographe.*

1968 Publishes historical biography *L'étrange croisade de l'empereur Frédéric II.*

1970 Publishes collection of short stories *Quia absurdum (sur la terre comme au ciel).*

1971 Publishes novel *Les jeux de l'esprit.*

1972 Publishes novel *Les oreilles de jungle.*

1974 Publishes novel *Les vertus de l'enfer.*

1976 Grand Prix de la Société des Gens de Lettres de France for his body of work. Publishes collection of stories *Histoires perfides.*

1978 Publishes novel *Le bon Léviathan.*

1979 Publishes novella *Les coulisses du ciel.*

1980 Final visit to l'Ilon.

1981 Publishes novel *L'énergie du désespoir.*

1982 Publishes novel *Miroitements.*

1983 Publishes novel *La baleine des Malouines.*

1985 Publishes novel *Pour l'amour de l'art.*

1987 Publishes essay on cosmology *L'univers ondoyant.*

1988 Publishes novel *Le professeur Mortimer.*

1990 Publishes novel *Le malheur des uns. . .* and autobiographical work *L'îlon.*

1992 Publishes novella *A nous deux, Satan!*

1994 Dies 30 January.

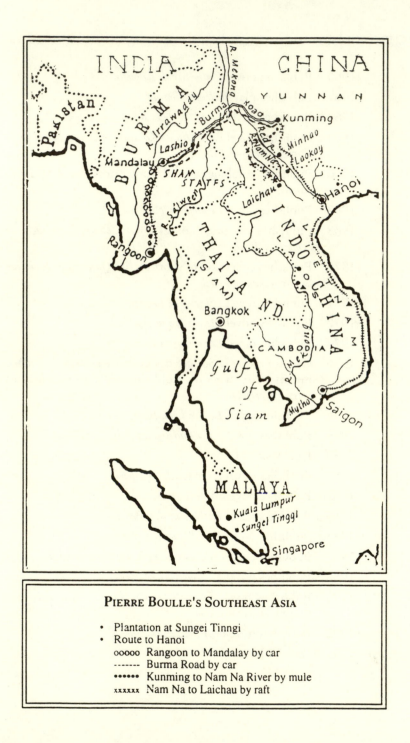

PIERRE BOULLE'S SOUTHEAST ASIA

- Plantation at Sungei Tinngi
- Route to Hanoi
  - ooooo Rangoon to Mandalay by car
  - ------- Burma Road by car
  - ••••• Kunming to Nam Na River by mule
  - xxxxxx Nam Na to Laichau by raft

Chapter One
Biography—An Uncommon Life

The first work of a novelist is often a bildungsroman—a novel that gives an account of the author's early years in the person of a fictional alter ego. But nothing is usual in the life and oeuvre of Pierre Boulle. His first novel, *William Conrad* (*Not the Glory*), 1950, takes place in an England he knew only through the writings of authors like Rudyard Kipling, Joseph Conrad, and Somerset Maugham, and through contacts with English colonists in Malaya. The story it recounts touches only peripherally on the author's experiences. Still, some recovery of childhood has often been an imperative for the writer, retrieving a portion of what he alone knows is still lying there in the wake of his years. In the case of Pierre Boulle, it was necessary to wait 40 years for his journey to his personal first land-scape—the autobiographical *L'îlon*, published when the author was 78 years old—which provides the key to what he calls the most important years of his life, the period of "exalted dreams" between the ages of 8 and 13. Here the author evokes images of these early years, eschewing, like Proust, strict chronology to follow the order of memory. These images, he writes, "with their mixture of joy, of anguish, of hope, and of disap-pointment, constitute a store of riches which I never tire of counting, as an old miser counts his coins."[1]

But, unlike the miser who hoards his wealth, Pierre Boulle shares his with his readers. With these images he gives us a picture of the Provence that formed him, one that we find in *La face* (*Face of a Hero*), 1953; and, much later, in *Le bon Léviathan* (*The Good Leviathan*), 1978; *Miroitements* (*Mirrors of the Sun*), 1982; and *A nous deux, Satan!*, 1992. While Boulle's resolutely serene boyhood is reminiscent of that of Marcel Pagnol, who, however, remained in his beloved Provence, Boulle's subsequent life of travel and adventure is like that of André Malraux. Details of the years between the ages of 24 and 38 can be found in *Le sacrilège malais* (*S.O.P.H.I.A.*), 1951, a fictionalized version of Boulle's experiences as a rubber planter in British Malaya from 1936 to 1939, and *Aux sources de la rivière Kwaï* (*My Own River Kwai*), 1966, an autobiographical account of his adventures as a Resistance fighter and secret agent in Indochina during World War II. And then, another abrupt change took place in

1

Boulle's life. From the age of 38 until his death in 1994, his life was like that of Gustave Flaubert; Boulle, too, retired from active life to devote himself exclusively to writing, thus transforming his biography into a bibliography. In the volumes comprised in this bibliography are reflected all of the influences and experiences of the first four decades of his life.

In the preface to *L'îlon,* Boulle refutes Kipling's assertion that the first six years are decisive in a boy's life. Boulle has very few memories of those years. For him, the decisive years, those covered in *L'îlon,* were between the ages of 8 and 13, which he describes as his "life as a little savage." The opening words of the volume support his contention: "I must have been eight or nine years old when my father told me, cautiously, as if taking great care to spare me a violent emotion, that he had purchased a small carriage, with a horse, and a country house on the banks of the Rhône river" (*L'îlon,* 9). L'Ilon was the name they gave to this property, a name probably derived from "îlot" (small island), for this isolated cottage overlooking the Rhône rose alone above the flooded bank when there was a rise in the level of the river. From the very first moment Boulle sensed that this was a special, magic realm. "When I think of this period, I wonder," he asks, "whether I had a normal childhood or whether I was a special case. Marcel Pagnol certainly had similar sensations and experiences, but he had a friend his age" (*L'îlon,* 169). Boulle, on the contrary, led a rather solitary life at l'Ilon in the company of a few adults. Even though he had school friends in Avignon, he became totally removed from them on Thursdays and Sundays in the enchanted domain of the Rhône river. When he invited them to l'Ilon, he realized that they did not share his fascination with the river and, by mutual consent, they never returned.

The most important person in this special world was his father, "the possessor of fabulous secrets" (*L'îlon,* 12), who imbued his son with his own love of nature. He was a brilliant lawyer whose legal world of Avignon is evoked by Boulle in *Face of a Hero.* Maître Boulle was also a man of letters, the author of newspaper articles and poetry as well as a play that was staged in Avignon. He even wrote a magazine for the immediate family and close relatives, which he read aloud to them, delighting them with his irony, a mode of literary expression that is a distinguishing characteristic of his son's work. Together with his literary gifts, Boulle's father passed on to him his two great passions, hunting and fishing.

When Boulle was 15 years old, his father died of endocarditis; his absence robbed l'Ilon of its attraction. In a final moving tribute, Boulle evokes in *L'îlon* the funeral of his beloved father and the words of the eulogy that echoed the belief of all who knew him that he had been the best of all men. "That was indeed my opinion," (*L'îlon*, 173) writes Boulle. His great love and admiration for his father led Boulle to emulate him by adopting his ironic, tolerant view of human foibles and weaknesses, together with a concomitant refusal to judge. He describes this as "some odd mental quirk" that has always prompted him to seek excuses for his enemies.[2]

His mother, Boulle writes, shared the belief that his father was the best of all men. "I know it," he continues, "because I saw her recently in a dream, when I had put the finishing touches to these images of the past, and I felt guilty about not having assigned her a more important role" (*L'îlon*, 173). But she told him that he had done well, that his father had indeed been the best of all men. Besides, she added, "those are men's affairs . . . I could only play a minor part in them" (*L'îlon*, 173). And, indeed, we find that almost all of Boulle's stories are about men. Women play supporting roles; they are portrayed, however, sympathetically, without a trace of misogyny. "Then you don't hold it against me," he remarks with relief to his mother in the dream, "that I didn't give sufficient praise, as I would have wanted, to you and the role you played at l'Ilon. It is because, as you well know, certain sentiments cannot be expressed in writing" (*L'îlon*, 174). This sense of modesty and restraint, as well as the use of litotes, which we find throughout Boulle's literary production, are very different from Provençal hyperbole and love of the tall story that are also in his work. These stylistic divergences, as well as the preoccupation with the dichotomy between good and evil within the human soul, can perhaps be explained by the duality within his father between the outstanding barrister of Avignon and the poacher and illegal hunter of l'Ilon.

It was with his father that Boulle shared the most thrilling experiences of his youth, hunting and fishing at l'Ilon, which, although situated only a few kilometers from Avignon, seemed to be very far away from civilization. One of the most memorable experiences of these early years, the only account Boulle gave of his youth before the publication of *L'îlon*, appeared in 1970 in a short story titled "L'affût au canard" ("The Duck Blind").[3]

"I was ten years old," the story begins. "In the winter my father and I used to drive out of town in a real carriage, with a horse. To save time my father would come to meet me when school let out" ("Duck," 77). If the weather was cold enough, his father would exclaim that it was right for the duck blind, and the boy would imagine as they rode along that he heard a sound "like the clicking of mechanical wings . . . magic music like no other natural phenomenon, portent of the approach of a flight of ducks at dawn" ("Duck," 78). At four o'clock in the morning, they would go out to the blind to spot them at "the moment when, fascinated by the tranquil waters of the pools, the ducks swoop down in a tumult of splashings" ("Duck," 80). For five years, they would repeat the ritual, spending freezing hours in the blind, and not once did they see a duck. "Not one single time did I hear the clicking of mechanical wings. . . . [Only once] as we were returning home, very high in the sky and well above the track of finches, thrushes, and starlings, we saw a magic triangle with dotted lines. In spite of the distance we could make out the stiff, outstretched necks of migratory birds and a supernatural vibration filled the air" ("Duck," 84). Since then, he concludes, "I have had many strange adventures. Since then I have invented others even stranger, but never have I felt such violent palpitations, never has my heart sounded so feverishly as in that icy blind on the banks of the Rhône at the hour of the duck" ("Duck," 84).[4]

In just a few pages, Boulle is able to convey the atmosphere surrounding an unforgettable experience of his early youth. He recognizes that this is characteristic of his style: "Do not expect me to give you a detailed portrayal of l'Ilon. I do not have a gift for description. I can only attempt to convey a few impressions" (*L'îlon,* 18). Or again, "as for the fragrances made up of immaterial vapors and scents which rose from the countryside, I was subject to their intoxicating influence for many years, but I am incapable of describing them"(*L'îlon,* 23). Boulle's strength lies not in description but in plot, for he is primarily a storyteller. Vignettes and anecdotes throughout *L'îlon,* in particular an anecdote about the feeding of the birds, reveal his exceptional narrative skills.

One day at l'Ilon, Boulle's father told him that, although their blind was perfect, they needed a collection of cages containing different types of birds, which could then attract other birds with their Circean songs as they flew by. Although there were certain whistles one could use, nothing was as effective as the true bird call. The author then describes their visit to one of his father's former legal clients to borrow some of his birds for this purpose. This man was not only a specialist in hunting birds from a blind but was also the owner of a bar cum brothel. The bar, which had its own entrance, was separated from the man's apartment by a wall with a single connecting door that was usually closed. When the boy and his father entered the apartment, the wife was feeding the birds. She opened the cages one by one, carefully took each bird into the hollow of one hand, and with the other hand filled the trough with seeds and put water into the cup. The bird never budged in her expert hands, but trembled and moved around frenetically once back in its cage. Because there were many birds, the feeding took a long time. From time to time one of the *poules* would come in and, under the indulgent gaze of the woman, would come to the table, put a timid finger between the bars of a cage, pat the bird gently, and whisper a few tender words to it. "I believe that that is the most vivid image I have kept of this initiation to hunting game from a blind," Boulle concludes, particularly "the look of wonder of the *poules,* who had come to seek there a bit of human warmth and a diversion in fondling the warm down of the occupants of the cages" (*L'îlon,* 43–44).

Second to Boulle's father in the magical world of l'Ilon was Pauleau, the archetypal Provençal. The Boulles' first meeting with him took place in a climate of suspicion engendered by Pauleau's contempt for the city dwellers, but his contempt disappeared when he discovered that the father was a connoisseur of the Rhône. From that day on, they became friends, and it was Pauleau who pronounced the brief eulogy at Eugène Boulle's funeral. Pauleau also loved to tell stories and was delighted to find a willing listener in the young boy. His favorite story was about his having caught a fish weighing 13 pounds. Boulle noted that each time he told his story, he embellished it with new details; the basic story, however, remained the same. Unlike other fishermen, who stretched their arms apart to show the great size of their catch, Pauleau never did so: "The magic of words was enough for him" (*L'îlon,* 62). Pauleau is the model, even down to the name, for the Provençal fisherman in *Mirrors of the Sun.* For the fictional namesake, as for the real Pauleau,

> life unfolded to a rhythm that would have pleased the most demanding ecologist: the rhythm dictated by the sun. His daily routine slightly exceeded the solar day. He rose at dawn, downed his coffee before leaving home—a plain wooden shack—and headed for the sandy shore where he had beached his rowboat the day before. After dragging it into the water, he would set out along one of the local waterways, tributaries of the Rhône, some of which served to irrigate rice paddies bordering the Crau Plain. If the channel was wide enough, he would reach for his oar; if not, he poled his small craft silently through the reeds and dwarf willows.[5]

Pauleau's tales were all recollections of past adventures, some described with accuracy, others embellished with dramatic details that made them at times extremely difficult to believe. Nonetheless, the young boy listened to all of them with equal interest. The stories appeared to have their starting point in reality—particularly those about World War I, poaching, fishing, hunting wild boar—but it was not long before Pauleau would give free reign to his "creative imagination, a tendency reinforced by his Provençal temperament" (*L'îlon*, 149). At times, he would tell the story of how, because of his reputation as an expert hunter, he had been chosen during the Great War to fire on enemy planes with his rifle, bringing down a good number in the process.

When listening to Pauleau's stories with their mixture of reality and fantasy, the young boy had to suspend disbelief until he came totally under their spell. This, too, is the way one must read the works of Pierre Boulle, who has remarked: "Every time I tell a story, the editor tells me it is implausible. But, subsequently, curiously, the reading public seems convinced that it actually happened."[6] But the story Boulle tells is not wholly the product of Provençal exaggeration; it is the tall story, tempered, however, by French scientific rationalism. It is a logical demonstration of a premise carried with insane rationality to an absurd conclusion.

Many experiences and adventures of his childhood reappear in Boulle's literary production. He describes in detail the hunting of larks with mirror-lures that figures later on in *Mirrors of the Sun*. The boy used to spend hours manipulating a string that twirled a mirror to attract larks in the vicinity. When the sun rose, the mirror began to sparkle and larks appeared one after the other, hypnotized by the sight. "They are doing the Holy-Ghost," his father would whisper to him (*L'îlon*, 68). Doing the Holy-Ghost means that the lark, with outspread wings, glides slowly above the mirror in lazy, graceful circles, making a target impossible to miss. The attraction of larks to mirror-lures causes the first in a series of contretemps that ultimately doom the great solar power station in *Mirrors of the Sun*, thereby illustrating Boulle's contention that nearly all great human achievements are destined to fail because of one little detail overlooked by their creators.

All life in the area of l'Ilon centered around the Rhône. Boulle adored the river in all of its aspects, "which varied from one season to the other according to the quirks of nature, particularly when its waters became dark and swollen with foam and carried along an accumulation of assorted rubbish" (*L'îlon*, 114). The house faced the Rhône, which flowed along peacefully a few meters below when it was at a reasonable level, but which receded at times when there was little rain, leaving a large dry space of dark silt and sparkling gravel. "But when storms and melted snow had swollen the Ardèche, the Isère, the Saône and many other mountain streams, when the dam formed by the waters of the Durance, which was also rising, slowed down the flow of the liquid mass downriver from Avignon, the Rhône changed character, color, and smell in a few days, sometimes in a few hours. It swelled, tossed about in eddies and violent whirlpools . . . rising almost to the level of the house which, fortunately, was raised. Sometimes it rose even higher" (*L'îlon,* 19–20).

Boulle was able to determine by the odors emitted by the river whether it was still calm or whether it had risen during the night, a faculty he lends to Major Shears in the last scene of *Le pont de la rivière Kwaï.* Boulle's intimate knowledge of every aspect of the Rhône influenced his decision early in World War II to infiltrate into French Indochina by descending the Nam-Na River on a raft, an experience he describes in *My Own River Kwai.* He reasoned that the Rhône had provided him with a certain amount of experience with rivers; he knew its treacherousness, its eddies, its sharp bends and its turbulent rapids between sheer cliffs. Unfortunately, as he was to learn, each river is different, and his past experience served him badly on this dangerous mission.

Boulle continued to go to l'Ilon for a few years after the death of his father, but he was no longer drawn to it. Soon after, the property was sold. He did go back much later, but he was too depressed to even go into the house, now occupied by others, and he vowed never to return. Despite this, he went back once more during the 1980s. The area was unrecognizable; the house had been razed and the site leveled. Even the Rhône, he notes, was no longer the same: "It is now hemmed in by dikes and flows quietly along the banks of a flat steppe covered with short grass. The willow plantations no longer exist. Along the entire right bank, not a tree, not a shrub, not a bush remain to catch the eye which can now see as far as the outskirts of Avignon, whereas in the past I moved about in a fairytale world in which I felt far away from the real world" (*L'îlon,* 176–77).

Not a single material object remained to inspire nostalgia. "I think it is better this way," Boulle concludes. "On discovering this foreign world, I gave a sigh of relief" (*L'îlon,* 177). The lost paradise of Boulle's childhood, consigned to his memory, now, like Proust's Combray, remains intact in the pages of his work.

Pierre Boulle left Avignon a few years after his father's death. Despite his great love and respect for his father, he did not feel that he was suited for the law and went instead to study science and engineering in Paris. The style and content of Boulle's fiction bear the mark of his scientific education; he attributes to it his "somewhat cruel taste for the bizarre together with great formal simplicity and rigorous logic" (Interview, 28 November 1992). It is also apparent in his essay on cosmology *L'univers ondoyant* (The undulating universe), 1987, and in his science fiction novels and short stories.

Boulle received his *licence ès sciences* in 1931, and spent the following year training as an electrical engineer at the Ecole Supérieure d'Electricité, where he received his diploma. After this, he worked as an engineer for a research organization in Clermont-Ferrand. The picture Boulle paints—in the autobiographical novel *S.O.P.H.I.A.*—of the company in France where he began his engineering career portrays it as "dismal, gloomy, and inhuman. . . . [a] setting of factory chimneys and corrugated iron roofs, veiled in black dust and shrouded in bitter memories"[7]; a setting calculated to exacerbate the tedium of his occupation. At this time, according to Boulle, he had a lot in common with Joyce—one of the protagonists of *The Bridge over the River Kwai*—a young volunteer in the dangerous commando unit Force 316 during World War II. In civilian life, Joyce had had a dull career as a draftsman in a big engineering firm.

> There were two dozen young men of the same age sitting all day long over their drawing boards in a common workroom. . . . When he wasn't drawing he was working out sums—with formulae and a slide rule. Nothing exciting. He doesn't seem to have liked this job very much . . . he seems to have welcomed the war as the chance of his lifetime. . . . His firm had to do with bridges, articulated bridges in metal—a standard model. They made them in separate pieces and delivered them all together to the contractors—just like a Meccano [erector] set. He was never out of the office. For two years before the war he drew the same piece over and over again . . . a girder. His job was to determine the shape that would give the greatest resistance for the smallest weight of metal. If it hadn't been for that girder, he probably wouldn't at this very moment be lying flat on his face in the undergrowth a hundred yards from the enemy, with a knife in his belt and an instrument of wholesale destruction by his side.[8]

Boredom and restlessness and a desire to travel led Boulle to ask the placement office at the Ecole Supérieure to contact him when there was a job abroad. Coincidentally, the Société Financière de Caoutchouc was looking for an electrical engineer for its plantations in Malaya. And so at the age of 24, in 1936, Pierre Boulle left Clermont-Ferrand to become a rubber planter in British Malaya, not knowing exactly what his functions would be; the personnel manager in Paris had told him that he might expect to be assigned to the fields for an indefinite period of time and that it was not even certain that his engineering qualifications would ever be put to use. "The Personnel Manager had stressed this point in somewhat forceful terms, as though to destroy in advance any illusions the young man might entertain on the value of his degree. Maille [Boulle] had raised no objection. His brief experience in industry in France had led him to feel a special esteem for agricultural work and an open-air life" (*S.O.P.H.I.A.,* 39).

A fictionalized account of Boulle's years in Southeast Asia can be found in his only autobiographical novel, *Le sacrilège malais* (*S.O.P.H.I.A.*), 1951, a title inspired by the *Sortilège malais* of Somerset Maugham, whom he greatly admired. In the pages of Boulle's novel we find atmosphere, local color, characters, and incidents that reappear in all of Boulle's novels and short stories set in the Orient: *Le pont de la rivière Kwaï* (*The Bridge over the River Kwaï*), 1952; *Le bourreau* (*The Executioner*), 1954; *L'épreuve des hommes blancs* (*The Test*), 1955; *Les voies de salut* (*The Other Side of the Coin*), 1958; *Les oreilles de jungle* (*Ears of the Jungle*), 1972; *Les vertus de l'enfer* (*The Virtues of Hell*), 1974; *Histoires perfides* (*The Marvelous Palace and Other Stories*), 1977; and *Le malheur des uns . . .* ("One man's joy . . ."), 1990. We find also in *S.O.P.H.I.A.* the genesis of one of the most important themes in all of Boulle's oeuvre, the inevitable corruption of human enterprise, as he traces the young man's initial infatuation with the corporation, his growing knowledge of its caprices, and final disillusionment as he comes to know it better.

The English title of the novel, *S.O.P.H.I.A.,* is the acronym for Society for the Overseas Promotion of Horticulture, Industry, and Agriculture, which came into being just before World War I. Contrary to all reasonable modus operandi, but typical of that of the organization, the founders of the corporation proceeded backwards; they found a satisfactory acronym first and then attempted to find a significant title that could be formed from the initials. Subsequently, when speaking of The S.O.P.H.I.A. Company, it became the custom to leave out the periods between the initials, then the article, then the word *Company,* until all that remained was the symbolic name Sophia. The personnel of the organization were divided into three groups: the working or "cobbler class" (*S.O.P.H.I.A.,* 10), exemplified by Ramasamy, the archetypal Tamil tapper, an unfortunate individual imported from India, where he was a pariah; the Chinese laborer, also imported, who was indispensable

because of his efficiency; and, finally, the native Malay, who did no work
and asked only to be left in peace but who, nevertheless, consented now
and then to perform tasks like driving a luxury automobile for Sophia.
Midway between the cobbler class and the one comprising the financial
tycoons in Europe was the corps of intermediaries, the planters, from
many European countries, but particularly from France and England,
drawn by the mysterious allure of a new enterprise in a country still covered by jungle.

When Boulle arrived in Malaya, he was sent to a plantation near
Kuala-Lumpur where he was employed initially as a rubber planter. The
opening pages of *S.O.P.H.I.A.* describe the arrival in Malaya of Boulle's
alter ago, Maille, on a stifling hot morning in December 1936. Maille, a
new recruit to Sophia, is met at the station of Kuala Getah, the capital of
Telanggor, by Reynaud, the company secretary who, despite the intense
heat, is wearing the office workers' uniform of white trousers, long-
sleeved shirt, collar, and tie (*S.O.P.H.I.A.,* 13). Maille exemplifies a type
of adventurous, romantic young man nurtured on the writings of
Kipling and captivated by the beauties of the jungle and the charm of
the natives.

> The Malayan world saw them disembark, suitcase in hand, in their
> European clothes, their eyes wide in expectation of some unlikely
> Eldorado. The Malayan world saw them, in their early days, toil along the
> steep paths, clamber up the hills, come to a stop at the limit of the plan-
> tation, and halt in awe, for no apparent reason, before the ramparts of the
> jungle. On occasion the Malayan world saw them peer furtively into the
> damp undergrowth at the foot of the giant trees, as though it was a for-
> bidden garden, and inhale the alien scent of humus. This would last a few
> months, during which their experience of the Malayan world extended no
> further. At the end of their first year they bought a car, for which Sophia
> let them have an advance. Then they gradually paid off the debt. They
> became economical. They began to think about their eventual retire-
> ment. They achieved promotion and applied their minds to symbolic fig-
> ures and abstract shapes. The crowning point of their careers consisted of
> sitting at a director's desk and spending most of their time in the office.
> They retired before they were fifty, after Sophia had extolled their loyalty
> to the Company in the course of an official gathering. Younger men took
> their places and the cycle continued. (*S.O.P.H.I.A.,* 227)

Maille is assigned to the Kebun Kessong plantation, one of the finest
of the company's plantations with 1 million first-class trees on 8,000
acres, in hilly country. It has four divisions, in each of which there is a vil-

lage of Tamil coolies, with shops, a hospital, a school, and an office. The plantation is under the direction of M. Loeken, a Belgian national, who instructs Maille in the rules of plantation life. He will need seven pairs of white shorts, a clean pair each day, some white suits for evening, and a motorcycle, for which money, to be repaid in monthly installments, will be advanced by the corporation. Roll call is held at four o'clock in the morning, although work cannot start until an hour later when the sun rises, but then "it would have lost its religious character and been reduced to the level of commonplace utility. It was a point that had not escaped Sophia's notice. This spiritual communion in the dark was intentionally endowed" with all the sacred value of holy writ" (*S.O.P.H.I.A.*, 38). On Sundays, however, the planters are permitted to sleep until six or seven. No familiarity is permitted with an Asiatic, whoever he or she may be. It is necessary to adopt a decent attitude with the clerks and the supervisors, always keeping one's distance, and never shaking hands with them. An Asiatic is not permitted to be seated in the presence of a European without permission. You cannot carry your own suitcase. No wine, only water with meals, and no alcohol until sundown. On Sundays a glass of beer is permitted with the curry. A Tamil "boy" must not serve dinner in his "bajuh" (native shirt) but in a white jacket. To maintain the planter's image, no siestas are permitted except on Sundays, after curry.

Almost immediately after his introduction to the strict rules governing all aspects of plantation life, Maille becomes aware of the energetic futility of the corporation and its personnel when he meets M. Chaulette, the managing director of Sophia. While all of Boulle's characters in *S.O.P.H.I.A.* have certain traits in common with their real-life counterparts, albeit transformed and embellished to suit the needs of the novel, his M. Chaulette, except for the pseudonym, appears almost exactly as he was in reality (Interview, 28 November 1992). In characteristic fashion, Boulle merely presents the man without authorial comment; detailing Chaulette's absurdities is sufficient to make the reader aware of the problem of action losing sight of its goals and becoming merely action for the sake of action. In *S.O.P.H.I.A.*, Boulle's alter ego, Maille, seems to take Chaulette's behavior in stride; the author revealed, however, that, in fact, the man's idiocies infuriated him (Interview, 28 November 1992).

M. Loeken is the victim of the most egregious of Chaulette's sudden, wild impulses, one of the many that will alienate Maille from corporate life over the years.[9] Loeken finally receives authorization to have a new bungalow built to replace the original decrepit dwelling in which he has been living. Chaulette dreams of creating "something unique of its kind

that . . . [will] leave a lasting impression" (*S.O.P.H.I.A.*, 52). He wants a
lofty site for the bungalow and sends Maille and Dassier, one of Loeken's
assistants, to find the best location for this bungalow on a spot high up
in the hills and to map out a road. They find an ideal spot on Bukit
Musang (Civet Cat Mountain), protected from the prevailing wind by
the slightly higher Bukit Taggar (Thunder Mountain), a steep, forbidding, inaccessible sugar-loaf peak. A week later, after a gang of Chinese
laborers under the supervision of Dassier and Maille has cleared the summit of Bukit Musang, leveled the ground, dug the foundations, and
widened the track leading up to the site, Chaulette decides that Bukit
Taggar would be a better site since it is the highest in the region. He
tells them to fill in the holes on Bukit Musang, to slice off the peak on
Bukit Taggar, and to get to work on a road there. Loeken is in despair
because all of the money allocated for the bungalow will be spent digging and filling in holes.

Chaulette then makes a whirlwind visit and decides to install an
indoor pool on the first floor. Since the site is too narrow for a pool, they
will have to trim the mountain down more, an "original task—digging
a crater on a deserted peak—[that] really fascinated the Chinese"
(*S.O.P.H.I.A.*, 91). Following that, Chaulette, whose report on his masterpiece has not been well received by the board of directors, calls to say
that the hole for the swimming pool must be filled in. "You've been a bit
hasty," he tells poor Loeken, "haven't you? Look now, just between ourselves, a pool in the middle of a bungalow—don't you find that a little
incongruous, a little . . . snobbish to say the least?" (*S.O.P.H.I.A.*, 94).

Then Chaulette proceeds to attack the idea of a three-story bungalow,
an idea that had also been his. A circular building to fit the now-circular
site will be the answer, he then decides, and this will entail enlarging the
site further. And so, on the summit of Bukit Taggar, immortalized by
the natives in a series of Malayan poems called pantoums[10] and rebap-
tized Bukit Gila, "the Mad Mountain; the mountain of Madmen, the
Mountain of Madness, or even the Mountain in the throes of Madness,"
(*S.O.P.H.I.A.*, 86) "there emerged on the summit of Bukit Taggar a geo-
metrical monstrosity of a hitherto unknown species that, to the Malay
world, appeared from afar like a sort of Roman amphitheater crowned
by a drunken god with an enormous Chinese hat" (*S.O.P.H.I.A.*, 101).
Further, the successive cutting operations reduced the summit of Bukit
Taggar to the level of Bukit Musang, without, however, affording the
advantage of its large flat surface (*S.O.P.H.I.A.*, 102).

The ultimate absurdity in the bungalow fiasco occurs when Chaulette, instructed by the chairman of the board to submit photographs of the "costly fantasy" that do not "stress its outlandish appearance" (*S.O.P.H.I.A.,* 112), sends two of the planters out on a aerial mission to photograph it from above. The planters entrusted with the mission are killed when their plane crashes into the side of a mountain.

Chaulette's passion for unreality, which Maille finds inexplicable, provides the young man with endless opportunities for reflection. Chaulette, however, merely exemplifies the character of the corporation—the real object of Boulle's irony—with its discipline and its bureaucracy, and its absurd insistence on imposing its methods without taking concrete reality into consideration. In *S.O.P.H.I.A.,* Boulle satirizes scientific management and the mania for organizing. As a result of the search for an abstract idea of formal perfection, the sense of reality disappears. Rituals are sufficient in themselves and become their own raison d'être. The rubber company has become so closely identified with its formal constraints that it has made them a basic requirement for employment; employees can no longer function without them. Boulle's experiences with corporate bureaucracy in Malaya explain his antipathy to anything that dehumanizes the individual as well as his fear that from this milieu a strange synthetic creature will finally emerge with no resemblance to the human race.

The board of directors of Sophia, which is interested in improving efficiency in tapping the rubber trees, sends M. Bedoux, a representative of Ratio,[11] a firm that uses a system of chronometry for the evaluation of human labor, to the plantation. M. Bedoux, "who was a technical engineer, a specialist in methods improvement, and a French member of the international firm of 'Ratio,' landed in the British possession of Malaya, a country where poets in sarongs immortalized the Universal Soul in the shade of the coconut trees, with a view to modernizing the tapping of *Hevea bresilensis,* by analyzing the movements of Ramasamy the Tamil tapper, and co-ordinating these into a stylized and economic pattern" (*S.O.P.H.I.A.,* 114).

M. Bedoux follows Ramasamy as he leans over the tree and removes the coil of yellowed latex that has coagulated all the way down the recently made spiral in the trunk. He puts that into his bag, then carefully removes a thin strip of bark and opens up a vertical ridge connecting the spiral to a small aluminum gutter fastened to the tree at an angle. From this gutter the liquid drains into a porcelain cup. Conscious

of being observed by four white men, including the director of the plantation and a stranger, Ramasamy sets out with a will, displaying his tal-
ents, and leaping about to demonstrate his enthusiasm. M. Bedoux
watches him closely, takes out his chronometer, and tells them that
Ramasamy's activity is appreciably decreased by these physical jerks. At
the same time, confident that by leaping around he has given sufficient
evidence of his efficiency, Ramasamy almost dozes off, "lost in some private daydream of his own as he moved at a snail's pace around the tree."
On seeing this, one of the directors shouts: "Ni, badoua, odi po!" ("Get
a move on, you stinking little pimp!") (*S.O.P.H.I.A.*, 116). M. Bedoux,
horrified, informs them that the Ratio method is free of such perpetual
reprimands, which only irritate the overseer and tire out the workman.

M. Bedoux continues to clock Ramasamy's movements, without realizing that the tapper is making fun of him with his wild gestures, as
Maille continues to observe them, amazed "at the depths of absurdity to
which a Tamil tapper's fantasy could descend when it came up against
the speculative reasoning powers of the West. He felt there was no new
extravagance in which Ramasamy could indulge in his grotesque distor-
tion of the pure gesture advocated by M. Bedoux. Yet each time,
Ramasamy drew on his primitive brain for some still more fantastic
interpretation" (*S.O.P.H.I.A.*, 147).

M. Bedoux attempts to give him yet another demonstration, going
through all the gestures, indicating the shortest distance between various given points. As might be expected, he merely goes through the
motions of tapping, drawing the chisel across the surface of the bark
without cutting into it. Then, Ramasamy, dutifully imitating M.
Bedoux, draws his chisel across the surface of the bark, taking great care
not to cut into it. Bedoux shouts that Ramasamy is supposed to tap the
tree, that he has only been going through the motions; to make him
understand, Bedoux seizes a chisel and drives it into the tree, making a
gash in the bark. From that moment on, Ramasamy performs zealously,
making hideous gashes, cutting off great chunks instead of the thin delicate strip he had previously detached with loving care. Bedoux, in
despair, asks Maille to help. Maille turns to the tapper and launches into
a furious diatribe: "Ni, pendi ni, surruka odi po" ("Get a move on you
swine, or you'll have me to reckon with!") (*S.O.P.H.I.A.*, 150).

A few days later, to his great delight, Maille sees Bedoux hitting and
cursing Ramasamy in demented frustration. Finally, a compromise is
reached between theory and practice: Ramasamy goes through the same

movements as before, only now he carries out his task in a series of fits and starts that give the illusion of speed.

During his months of apprenticeship at Kebun Kossong, Maille feels that in Sophia he has really found the best of all corporate enterprises. The mild restraints imposed on the personnel are compensated for by material advantages and by the fascination of working as a team. Also, free of major responsibilities at his level, he has an opportunity to appreciate the enchantment of a planter's life in Malaya:

> the immensity and mysterious majesty of the equatorial jungle seen from the summit of Bukit Taggar; the strange smell of mold it gave out when it suddenly came into view round a bend in the mountain track, like an impenetrable wall marking the boundary of the civilized world; the motorcycle rides over the hills; the downpours that within a few minutes turned dry river beds into raging torrents, while the wind brought the rubber trees toppling down across the roads; the brilliant sunshine that inevitably followed storm or gale; the blanket of mist that formed on some mornings halfway up the mountains; the dark mass of the artificial forest at nighttime, with the fireflies that made the darkness seem all the more intense; the musical whimpering of the monkeys at dawn; and even the silence of the bungalow in the evening, after the passage of the flying foxes had given the signal to retire. All these attractions, perceptible only to a mind at peace, could still be enjoyed by those on the first rung of the ladder. (*S.O.P.H.I.A.*, 88–89)

When his period of probation is over, Maille is transferred to the technical department and receives a contract for a salary of 250 Straits dollars a month plus an allowance for a houseboy and a motorcycle, with increases in pay at the company's discretion and a possible bonus at the end of the year. He must agree to remain unmarried for at least two years and obtain special permission from the company before marrying during the two following years. Six months home leave is granted every four years, passage paid, second class for the assistants, first for the managers. The contract can be terminated by either party with one month's notice, but, in the case of grave misdemeanor on the part of the employee, the company reserves the right of instant dismissal, with no indemnity or guarantee of a passage home (*S.O.P.H.I.A.*, 103–4). Financial security for life!

Maille, however, is becoming more and more restless. During his probationary period there had been one or two attempts against his individual liberty that he had resented at first, but, after comparing them with some of his experiences in Europe, he concluded that they were not very serious. Now he finds many aspects of his new life oppressive, among them the problem of sexual constraint. Sophia was on its guard against carnal desire and its sometimes unpredictable consequences. There were no beautiful maidens of tropical fantasy, but only shopworn prostitutes in brothels run by Japanese ladies or taxi girls from the dance halls. Finally, there was always the Tamil cook's wife, who "did not behave like a savage. She was careful not to spit on the floor when she was in the master's bedroom. When she took off the length of cloth that served as her dress, she also removed the quid of betal she had been chewing since dawn and that gave her teeth the same color as her skin. . . . Through lack of enthusiasm the cook's wife was incapable even of simulating pleasure. . . . There were several other drawbacks . . . she left a smell of coconut oil on everything she touched, and the room stank of it for hours afterward" (*S.O.P.H.I.A.,* 138–39).[12]

For many other reasons, Maille is finding Malaya less attractive since his promotion and his transfer to the technical staff section. He no longer has the sensation of living in the Far East. Some of the symptoms that alarmed him during his early career in Europe now begin to reappear. There is no time to enjoy the beauties of Malaya. "During the day they were harassed by Company affairs. At night they sought relief in alcohol. In the heart of Malaya they had recreated the European way of life" (*S.O.P.H.I.A.,* 156). Maille tries to determine the exact cause of his depression and realizes that it stems from an incident that occurred two days before. He had written a 10-page report on a series of experiments he had undertaken in the technical department laboratory on the manufacture of special types of rubber. By incorporating varying quantities of chemical ingredients into the latex, he obtained a number of different products, some harder, others softer than the ordinary rubber. He was excited about his discovery and disheartened when the report reappeared on his desk, unread, with instructions to retype it in capital letters to conform to Sophia's prescribed format. Typing took precedence over intellectual endeavor.

Collective work, with all the artificiality, constraint, and degradation for the individual that its inevitable organization entails becomes increasingly more onerous to Maille, who begins to develop a real hatred for the team spirit. The Europeans learn nothing other than what relates to the organization; they neither know anything about the Malay world that exists beyond the plantation nor speak the language of the country. There may be times in the beginning when the collective effort does seem worthwhile, but it always deteriorates. Boulle's experience as a planter in Malaya is the source of a basic theme in his oeuvre—the inevitable subverting of all human enterprise.

The outbreak of war throws the planters of Malaya into a state of feverish anticipation of a change in their own existence, a feeling akin to the one that had brought them to Malaya. They belong to that small minority who happened one day not only to dream of adventure but also to make a decision to realize that dream. That is why they are there. Once they arrived, however, their individual will was too quickly blunted to break away, and even if they had felt an urge to do so they would have suppressed it for emotional as well as for financial reasons. "The war had put an end to this state of things. For many of them it appeared, though they would not admit it, as a heaven sent opportunity to achieve their freedom without a twinge of conscience, since leaving was implicitly a patriotic duty to which even Sophia would be forced to acquiesce" (*S.O.P.H.I.A.,* 228). Despite Sophia's efforts to obtain a deferment for him, Maille refuses and offers his resignation. To the exhilaration of his newfound liberty is added the joy of having won it himself by suddenly recovering his sense of independence. His resignation, however, is not accepted; instead he is placed on leave for the duration of the war.

Boulle recounts in *S.O.P.H.I.A.* the experiences of several of the planters of Malaya during World War II, but his own adventures are passed over briefly in the novel. Although he wrote his memoirs of that period shortly after the end of the war, he published them only in 1966 under the title *Aux sources de la rivière Kwaï* (*My Own River Kwai*), in order to explain the genesis of his most famous novel, *The Bridge over the River Kwai:*

> For a long time I vainly tried to elucidate this mystery, which was as irritating for myself as for . . . [the reader]. If the source of the *details* is obvious, where on earth could I have found the general idea, the *background,* which to me is essential? Well, I believe I have solved the problem. The background is likewise contained in this series of adventures. . . . [Here] I merely give the *narrative* after the *novel,* while stating that the one contains in a diffuse state all the material, all the spiritual substance of the other. This, more than any real explanation, will perhaps shed some light on my intuitive conception of the art of fiction. (*My Own,* 8–9)

The detailed account of his wartime adventures, more exciting than any of his works of fiction, as well as a narrative of World War II in

Southeast Asia, can be found in *My Own River Kwai*. In the foreword to these memoirs, Boulle states that he tried to recall as faithfully as possible his wartime adventures in the Far East, starting at the moment of the declaration of war when he was a rubber planter in Malaya:

> The first part covers a period of "normal" mobilization in Indo-China, whither I had been summoned like many other Frenchmen. . . . It was only after July, 1941, when I returned to Singapore and joined Free France, that events took a more exciting turn for me: for me and a few others, mostly planters, a small group of Frenchmen exiled at the other end of the earth and kept in a permanent state of restlessness by the equatorial sun, the upheavals in Europe . . . and . . . a natural tendency to impetuosity and ebullience, the very tendency perhaps that had drawn us to Malaya in the first place. We were romantics. The course of the war, the series of disasters that had overwhelmed our country, assumed in our eyes an element of wonder that was even more fabulous and tragic for anyone listening to the news in a plantation tucked away in the middle of the jungle, and cruelly conscious of his isolation and helplessness. It is therefore not surprising that when the war spread to Southeast Asia our first reaction was a feeling of hope: at least we were not to be eternally excluded from the epic. Nor should it be held against us that our ambitions were exaggerated and that the schemes we contemplated hardly tallied with our capacities. We were romantics: amiable, touching, bumptious and probably incurable romantics. (*My Own*, 7–8)

In 1939, like all the French in the area except for Jean de Langlade, the current director of the company whose duties kept him in Malaya for the moment, Boulle was called up and posted to Indochina. He was sent first to Saigon and then to the Military Training Center at Mytho, where he taught Annamite soldiers how to march in step and shoulder a piece of bamboo instead of a gun, and from there to Hué, where the training program was the same as at Mytho. He became exasperated, for it seemed obvious to him that these peasants would never make soldiers. In a footnote in which he disparages his early colonialist ideas, Boulle remarks wryly: "On rereading these notes, it looks as if I was much mistaken on this point as on many others. They have learned to fight since those days—against us" (*My Own*, 23). It was also during this period that Boulle came into contact with the mountain tribes, so different from the lowland Annamites, who play an important role in the novel *Ears of the Jungle*.

After the French surrender in June 1940, Governor General Catroux, who had been negotiating an agreement with the British for the defense of Indochina, was replaced by the Vichyite Admiral Decoux. It became increasingly clear that Indochina favored the Vichy government, causing Boulle to think about escape to Malaya. But it was not until two years later, in July 1941, that he was finally able to embark for Singapore, "feeling almost light-hearted, so eager was I to escape this painful atmosphere of resignation and defeatism" (*My Own,* 39).

In Singapore, Boulle rejoined de Langlade, who had finally left Malaya, and enlisted with the Free French. Boulle's description of this incident is significant, for it provides a key to his honorable character. Rather than engaging in self-glorification or extolling his patriotism, Boulle notes that he does not know what exactly was his state of mind when he enlisted. Nor does he know "what proportions there entered into this decision of patriotism and a sense of duty on the one hand and, on the other, pride and the selfish prospect of experiencing elating and unusual adventures" (*My Own,* 43). This, he adds, is a question he will never be able to answer. What he does know, however, is that his enlistment marked the beginning of a series of adventures that were to have a marked effect on his life.

De Langlade was sure that war between the Allies and Japan was imminent and that Southeast Asia would become an important theater of operations. The reconquest of Indochina was an ideal for the Free French; their plan was to prepare a fifth-column organization with a view to sabotaging Japanese installations on the day the war was declared against the Allies. To this end—and here we have the genesis of Joyce's mission in *The Bridge over the River Kwai*—Boulle was invited by Force 136, the British organization dealing with enemy installations abroad, to take a course at the Convent, the name given to a special school situated in the jungle, where "solemn gentlemen methodically instructed us . . . in the art of blowing up a bridge, fixing an explosive charge to the side of a ship, derailing a train and also putting an end to an enemy sentry as silently as possible . . . [either by] slitting his throat with a knife [or] . . . bashing him over the head with a club" (*My Own,* 46). This was the problem that confronted Joyce in the crucial final scene of *The Bridge over the River Kwai.* At Force 136, officers were trained in the paramilitary activities of infiltration, exfiltration, demolitions, nighttime parachute jumps, and other clandestine operations. Boulle's knowledge of and experience with intelligence operations are reflected in *Not the Glory* and *Un métier de seigneur* (*A Noble Profession*), 1960.

The attack on Pearl Harbor in December 1941, as well as the events that followed, put an end to any possibility of carrying out clandestine operations in Indochina from a base in Singapore. Now begins for Boulle a series of adventures more thrilling than those of any of his fictional characters. De Langlade determines that he and Boulle will parachute into Indochina to organize a fifth column there, a plan that proves to be impracticable because of the lack of airplanes. Instead, they decide to transfer the mission to China, probably to Kunming, the capital of Yunnan province, proceeding by way of Rangoon. Boulle writes that he was elated at the prospect of getting to know the famous Burma Road, the Road to Mandalay that had been haunting him ever since he read Kipling's exhortation: "Come you back, you British soldier, come you back to Mandalay" (*My Own*, 60). We were frightful colonialists, Boulle comments in footnotes here and throughout the book.

Their departures are staggered, with Boulle and de Langlade disguised as Englishmen named Rule and Long, a measure that is necessary because the Chinese and Chiang Kai-shek still refuse to recognize Free France. Boulle makes one last stop in Malaya. In an almost deserted Kuala Lumpur he calls on J. Nicol, who has replaced de Langlade as director of the company and who is getting ready to move off at short notice, taking the company archives with him in a huge trunk.[13] The description of Boulle's last visit to the plantation, with the Japanese only a few miles away, sets the stage for the opening scene of the novel *The Test*.

At last the moment of departure arrives; Boulle embarks on a hydroplane to Rangoon, where he waits for word to enter China. The authorization he finally receives specifies that he has to supply his own transportation. The problem is solved when a call comes for a volunteer to drive the British consul's Buick to Kunming. Fearful that the offer may be rescinded, Boulle starts out immediately, without money or visa.

On January 30, 1942, with a British passport and afflicted with an accent which betrayed him as a native of the Vaucluse, without any valid papers, without even having enough money (an indispensable safe-conduct in China), Peter John Rule, born in Mauritius and British by birth through the machinations of the British and Chinese secret services combined, following in the wake of numerous American convoys towards Mandalay, towards China, almost towards Tibet and the Himalayas, sallied forth on the conquest of Indochina with a miniature revolver in his pocket and at the wheel of a motor car which would not have been out of place on the Riviera. The memory of that moment was to console me for many a subsequent disappointment. (*My Own*, 58–59)

At the wheel of his Buick, Boulle takes a scenic trip on the Burma Road from Mandalay to Lashio, passing through the Shan states, the center of the opium trade of the Golden Triangle, winding along the sides of sheer cliffs, through 3,000-meter-high passes. The trip provides the background for the thrilling voyage described in *The Virtues of Hell,* when the protagonist takes a shipment of heroin on a 600-mile mule trek through the mountains of Burma to the banks of the Salween River.

> I stopped a few miles above Mandalay, which was dominated by sheer cliffs bathed in a marvellous light. In the distance I could see the immensity of the Burma Plain, with its green paddy fields bordering the Irrawaddy. The huge South-Asiatic range started abruptly at my feet and extended above my head into other loftier, more chaotic, more mysterious mountains. . . . The next stop was Lashio, the last big town in Burma. . . . From Mandalay to Lashio I crossed the Shan States, the wildest part of Burma. . . . Lashio lies at an altitude of over three thousand five hundred feet. . . . From the Burma Road I was able to see . . . one of the loveliest landscapes in South-East Asia. It was an endless succession of precipices, peaks, saddles, smiling valleys, and waterfalls. (*My Own,* 60–63)

After driving for five days, Boulle finally arrives in Kunming, covered with dust and starving because he used all of his money to buy gas. There, together with de Langlade, Boulle helps to lay the foundations of Free France in China. A decision is made to have Boulle and de Langlade leave for the Tonkin frontier; they are to try to reestablish contact with friendly elements in the interior and to later enter Indochina themselves if circumstances permit. The Chinese have promised to provide wireless transmitters and operators as well as an interpreter and a guide. As they wait for the men and material to arrive from Chungking, Boulle and de Langlade spend their time becoming acquainted with the country and its inhabitants, learning all the mysteries of Chinese courtesy. To maintain the fiction of their identity as Englishmen they avoid all Frenchmen and speak only English, even using an interpreter and forcing themselves to remain impassive to his French translations, which are always completely inaccurate.

Finally, they are commissioned to leave for the frontier to make contact with the French Resistance in Indochina. They set off with an interpreter, two Chinese wireless operators, a guide, and an armed military escort in a caravan consisting of six mules for the baggage, a horse for

each member of the team, and two porters on foot to carry the transmit-
ter. After five days of climbing, they arrive at Pin-Ku-Yin, a military post
high up in the mountains, not far from the northern border of Tonkin, "a
merciless spot, a crag perpetually shrouded in mephitic mists, a mountain forsaken by man and God alike" (*My Own,* 93), which provides the
décor and sinister ambiance for *The Executioner.* Pin-Ku-Yin is situated at
the top of a pass. It is shrouded in clouds two days out of three. An icy
damp creeps into everyone and everything and has gradually rotted
away the thatch roofs of the huts, populated by demonic hordes of rats,
which also reappear in *The Executioner.* The Chinese probably chose Pin-
Ku-Yin as the ideal place to hide them away until the end of the war, but
they are not willing to do so and decide to move their base to an isolated
hamlet near Muong-La, a Thai village situated on the banks of the
Nam-Na river, only a few miles from the frontier. There they spend several months in vain efforts to make contact with like-minded Frenchman
in the border garrisons, during which time they experience great frustration in dealings with the various Chinese detailed by Chiang Kai-shek's
military authorities to help them. Boulle, sorely depressed, reflects that
he has done nothing but move from one place to another ever since the
outbreak of the war, traveling around a large circle whose center is situated somewhere in Siam (Thailand); now he is back at the gates of
Indochina with only a few steps needed to complete the circle.

Frustrated in their desire for action, Boulle and de Langlade finally
revert to Boulle's original plan: to descend the Nam-Na on a vessel of
some sort, then reach the Black River, then the Red River to Hanoi,
where they will find friends to help and protect them. Boulle decides to
attempt the journey himself when de Langlade is recalled to London to
take up a senior appointment there. After careful preparations, Boulle
embarks on a raft he has constructed of bamboos held together by rush-
es. He plans to travel by night, carried along by the current, and sleep
by day, sheltered by the forest. His baggage consists of civilian clothes,
money, a few letters to make contact with the Resistance, a list of the
bridges and engineering texts on the Hanoi-Saigon railway line, a manual on modern methods of sabotage, and five copies of a French-Chinese
glossary that is to serve as a code, all hermetically sealed in the water-
proof inner tube of a truck tire.

Every incident of his strange voyage was so deeply engraved on
Boulle's memory that he was able to describe it much later in minute
detail and incorporate it into Joyce's raft trip in *The Bridge over the River*

Kwai. Boulle tells about walking barefoot on razor sharp rocks as he is devoured by leeches and ants; being swept along by the current and hurled against the banks at every bend of the river; wandering at night in paddy fields up to his knees in mud; becoming disoriented when the current turns his raft around, moving him downstream backwards until he is caught up in whirlpools and spun around like a top and then dragged with his raft to the bottom of the river during a typhoon; then turning in endless circles in foam flecked waters with nothing but eddies, whirlpools, and geysers that fling him from bank to bank. And, through it all, he is always soaking wet and overcome with loneliness.

On the fifth day of this terrifying voyage, Boulle is stopped by Thai peasants and handed over to the French authorities at Laichau. He reveals his identity to Major F., who not only refuses to help him, but also arrests him and has him transferred to Hanoi, stating that he is and will always be loyal to Marshal Pétain, head of the Vichyite French government, and that the Free French are acting against the interests of France. Boulle notes that he "never felt any sterile resentment against Major F. It was my own fault and not his that I had gone so far as to imagine he had the same ardor and enthusiasm as we. Yet I have since heard that he has never forgiven me!" (*My Own,* 166). The irony of this situation must surely have pleased Boulle.

Boulle has now come full circle. He is back in Indochina, which he left about a year before. "After making a long detour through several countries in Asia, I was almost back where I had started from, flanked by two guards. The great adventure was over; it had ended badly, in utter defeat" (*My Own,* 168). Boulle is court-martialed by the Vichy colonial regime in October 1942, found guilty of treason, reduced to the ranks, deprived of French nationality, and sentenced to hard labor for life, which, ironically, keeps him from participating in the war against the Nazis. The first year of his imprisonment is very hard because the warders are anti-Gaullist and make life difficult for Boulle and two other Gaullist prisoners. Their treatment improves after the American landing in North Africa in November 1942, but deteriorates once again after the daring escape from of one of the Free French prisoners, Eugène Robert. Robert remains hidden in a safe house from which he is to be smuggled out the next night, but he is betrayed by a French colonel to whom an agent has carelessly revealed the hiding place, "a French colonel who had not merely refused to help him but had picked up the telephone to denounce him to the General Headquarters at Hanoi. . . . I never discovered if the colonel cashed in on the reward of five hundred piastres. The philosopher I have since become still hopes to be enlightened on this point one day" (*My Own,* 184).

According to Pierre Boulle, the French colonel who betrayed Robert, as well as the colonel who presided over Boulle's court-martial and sentenced him to hard labor for life, inspired the character of Colonel Nicholson in *The Bridge over the River Kwai.* Like Colonel Nicholson, both had a conception of honor that caused them to collaborate enthusiastically with the enemy at the expense of their compatriots. To these two might be added the medical officer who returned the dying prisoner Dr. Béchamp to the prison cell he shared with Boulle, where he could not receive proper treatment, just because another Gaullist prisoner had attempted to escape. "A Medical Officer is a sort of king, absolute master of his own domain" (*My Own,* 186), yet this one yielded without a murmur to an order from the Residency and the Government House. He banished from his hospital a patient, Dr. Béchamp, who was to die less than a month later for want of proper treatment. In *The Bridge over the River Kwai,* Boulle presents the antithesis of the medical officer responsible for Béchamp's death in the person of the heroic doctor Major Clipton.

During this time, having nothing to do—for, ironically, no job is assigned to this man sentenced to forced labor for life—Boulle begins to write to pass the time. On little bits of paper filched here and there, he scribbles some recollections of his adventures during the raft trip on the Nam-Na as well as a diary. When his captors search him and confiscate the papers, he rewrites what he has written, for he remembers every detail. When the Americans land on Sicily, the prisoners receive better treatment; when Allied victory appears certain, many new "friends" and "allies" suddenly materialize. In September 1944, after Boulle has spent two years and four months in prison, the prison authorities decide to organize the patriots' "escape," which is engineered with the connivance of all except for Admiral Decoux. They finally reach Free French headquarters in Calcutta, where Boulle celebrates his liberation, "paradoxically gloomy and depressed" (*My Own,* 211), feelings he had never had in prison.

Sick with malaria and dysentery, Boulle returns to Paris on 3 January 1945, after nine years of absence. From there, he goes to Avignon, to the home of one of his sisters—his mother died during the German occupation—to recuperate and to confront the problems of readjustment faced by those whose lives have been derailed by war.

What happens after the tumultuous elation of the turmoil depends on the intensity of the emotions experienced, on the degree to which the mind has been affected and on the particular manner in which each individual reacts to the return to normality, his ears still buzzing at night with persistent memories. Some, incurably intoxicated by the philter they have drunk, try for all they are worth to prolong the spell. They rush with a sort of desperation in pursuit of further adventures, more often than not to be disappointed, in a period of renewed peace that does not lend itself to this quest. Others, the greater number, recover, either willingly or reluctantly, the equilibrium of normal life. This is what I personally tried to do. I came back to France after an absence of nine years and, after a long spell of leave, returned to Malaya where a pleasant career awaited me, an organization that afforded less and less room for flights of fancy and a guaranteed pension at the end of so many years. (*My Own,* 212)

Boulle returns to Malaya because he does not know what else he can do. He has no plans, no desires, and therefore attempts to resume his life where the war had interrupted it. But he is unable to follow this sensible course, for the war has made him incapable of doing an ordinary job. For a while he refuses to admit this and struggles against it. Like the soldier in Hemingway's "Soldier's Home" who comes back from World War I, experiences the suffocation of civilian life, and tries to disengage himself from the world, "He did not want any consequences. He did not want any consequences ever again. He wanted to live along without consequences. . . . He wanted his life to go smoothly."[14]

A marvelous epiphany puts an end to Boulle's torment. He playfully itemizes the pressing reasons that made him realize that he was "clearly appointed by Destiny to make a name for . . . [himself] in Literature":

In the first place, I had had a scientific education. I had a bent for mathematics, theoretical physics, astronomy and, above all, cosmology. Secondly, I had started life as an electrical engineer, then I had been a rubber planter. Finally, my knowledge of literature was mediocre, almost non-existent as far as contemporary authors were concerned. . . . I read very little, and novels not at all. Essays bored me to tears . . . I tell you, it would have been crazy to hesitate a moment longer. It was an instant revelation. This was the course I had to take, and at once, without waiting another second. (*My Own,* 212–13)

Boulle immediately wrote a letter of resignation to the company for which he worked in Malaya, went back to Paris, sold all his possessions, moved into a little hotel on the Left Bank, and started writing a novel,

taking a vow to undertake nothing else ever again. Like his mentor
Joseph Conrad, who abandoned his career in the British Merchant Navy
for a writer's career, Boulle also gambled and won. Whether or not
Conrad's action prompted Boulle's[15] is less important than Boulle's
admiration for Conrad, which he expressed by naming his first novel
William Conrad and centering it about a putative Polish refugee from the
Nazis who acquires in a few years a leading position in English literature.
Boulle spent two years in financial misery writing *William Conrad* before
sending it off to Julliard, which published it, thereby launching his writ-
ing career.

"I have kept my word," Boulle writes at the end of *My Own River
Kwai*. "I have done practically nothing else ever since, and this foolhardy
decision, taken some twenty years ago among the fireflies piercing the
equatorial darkness of a Malayan plantation, still strikes me today as the
worthy conclusion to a series of incongruous adventures" (*My Own,* 214).

Chapter Two

Transformation of a Man

The human capacity for self-delusion has always fascinated Pierre Boulle. The transformation that takes place in a man as he identifies with the persona he has created is a dominant theme that is developed in different ways throughout his oeuvre, most remarkably in his tour de force *The Bridge over the River Kwai*. From his first novel, *William Conrad* (*Not the Glory*), to his last *Le malheur des uns . . .* , Boulle portrayed characters who are driven by what he calls "the demon of perversity," an incomprehensible inner force that pushes them to do what they should not do, inevitably acting against their own interests.

Not the Glory takes place in wartime London. Although Boulle had never been to England, the view of the English national character and English manners and customs he presents was based in part on his experience with British planters in Malaya who, he maintains, were not the slightest bit changed by being transplanted to the colonies:

> They're utterly impervious to local environment, and even after several years haven't acquired a single Oriental habit or vice. The Singapore banks are like the banks in London. The shops are like the shops in London. The clubs are like any English club, except for the fans. The members even dress like Englishmen, though their clothes are a little bit lighter than they would be at home. Everyone wears a tie, and I'm told that even in the most remote plantations people change for dinner every evening. From all this I draw the obvious conclusion that the English are insensible to any surroundings apart from . . . [their] own.[1]

Even more than by personal observation, Boulle's view of the English was influenced by the novelist Joseph Conrad, a debt made apparent by the novel's title, *William Conrad,* and the name of its eponymous hero. Boulle's protagonist resembles in many respects Joseph Conrad, who had seen in his native Poland a country vanquished by imperialism and who had found in England a nation at the height of its imperial power, proudly ruling the greatest empire the world had ever known. Conrad responded with admiration to the glamour, the moral assumptions, and the romantic hubris of the endeavor. Like many other Poles, he was an

Anglophile, regarding Britain as a land that reconciled tradition, stability, and respect for individual liberties and accepting without qualification the image of the "English gentleman," reticent, honorable, firm, keen on "fair play"; in short, an officer and a gentleman.

Boulle's protagonist, like Joseph Conrad, had assumed British nationality, adopted English as his language, and achieved a leading position in English literature and in public life. After fleeing from Nazi persecution in his native Danzig, Boulle's William Conrad became a heroic figure in wartime England. At the time of the German advance in Europe in 1940, William Conrad was a captain. Pinned down with the rest of his unit in a village in Flanders, he resisted until the last hand grenade and then succeeded in escaping with what remained of his men. Completely cut off from his headquarters, he managed to seize an enemy ammunition dump, after some desperate hand-to-hand fighting, and helped cover the English withdrawal from Dunkirk, where he was badly wounded. His feats of heroism on the field of battle, for which he was awarded the Military Cross, are later repeated in London, when he risks his life to save a child caught under the rubble of a bombed-out building. This exploit, reminiscent of much romantic fiction, is carried out, of course, by "a dashing man of action who could always adapt himself to the most unlikely situations" (*Glory*, 34).

After he is invalided out of the British army, William Conrad is called upon to advise the British War Ministry and assume the post of minister of propaganda. Applauded by an admiring public, Conrad wins the adulation of all, particularly Lady Goodfellow, wife of Sir Wallace, the archetypal British aristocrat, member of Parliament and chairman of the National Recovery League. But, in a development that adds the interest of a detective novel to a novel of customs and manners, the author reveals that Conrad is under surveillance by the British Intelligence Services, who have been alerted to the disappearance in Poland of a Nazi agent whose description tallies in many ways with his. All of Conrad's movements and correspondence are being monitored by the head of intelligence services.[2]

The reader soon discovers that the suspicions of British intelligence are accurate; Conrad is a loyal Nazi who has been planted in England to sabotage the war effort. Little by little, however, Conrad changes, and Boulle devotes the major part of the novel to tracing in detail his protagonist's psychological evolution as he is transformed from Nazi fanatic to British patriot under the pressure of circumstances. At first, Conrad, the German who has been trained to worship strength, force, and violence, feels pity for the English, whom he scorns as naive amateurs. But when he becomes minister of propaganda he gets caught up in the game and loses himself in his role. It then becomes a matter of self-esteem for him to demonstrate the superiority and efficacy of his methods, as it is with Colonel Nicholson in *The Bridge over the River Kwai* (see *Kwai*, 3). The day Churchill compliments him on his achievements, he is "overwhelmed with pride" (*Glory*, 191). Henceforth he hardly needs to pretend; he feels at home in his role. He can no longer hate the English, for he vibrates with their collective soul. When they sing "God Save the King," he is forced to recognize his defeat. His mentors had taught him how to protect himself against all sorts of physical and mental violence, but they had overlooked "the sweet, insidious influence of ordinary everyday impressions" (*Glory*, 217). Conrad is won over by the British "atmosphere of virtue" (*Glory*, 232) and realizes that if there is any justice in the world it is to be found in England, on the side of his former enemy. Once convinced of this, this "silly romantic ass" (*Glory*, 234) decides quite simply "to sacrifice his youth, talent, and life's blood in the cause of liberty!" (*Glory*, 233).

In a reversal as difficult to accept as many others that occur throughout Boulle's work, this Nazi agent in England becomes what he has pretended to be; he identifies with the persona he has created and reenlists in the British army, arranging to be posted to the Western Desert in a tank regiment. Again, as previously at Dunkirk, his heroism becomes legendary; virtually single-handedly, he turns the tide of battle at El Alamein, transforming a critical situation into a brilliant victory. William Conrad's exploits call to mind those of Joseph Conrad's protagonists, for, like his mentor, Boulle poses adult moral questions in terms of heroic, often adolescent, adventures. At the end of the novel, Colonel William Conrad, struck fatally by enemy bullets, remains conscious long enough to rejoice at having made the supreme sacrifice by dying like a hero for the cause of his country. Conrad's final action provides the key to the English title of the novel, which Boulle took from a maxim by Goethe and also used as the epigraph to the novel: "The deed is everything, not the glory."

Not the Glory shows the defects of a first novel; among them clichés that would enchant any admirer of Kipling, endless details about code solving and cipher breaking, and more information than the reader could ever wish to know about the stereotypical British national character. Boulle himself mentioned that he would like to change certain things in the novel, particularly the stylistic and emotional excesses of the scene in which the movie audience stands up as one at the end of a film presentation to sing "God Save the King" (Interview, 28 November 1992), as a "shimmering picture" (*Glory,* 151) of King George appears on the screen. "For the second time that week William Conrad went through the delirious experience of a mystic revelation. . . . As his own free will melted away, he felt himself seized heart and soul by the spirit of the crowd, the spirit of the crowd struggling desperately for existence in an infinity of possible combinations" (*Glory,* 153).

Still, when the novel was reissued in 1992, Boulle left it unchanged. Perhaps it was to show the way things were, the sentiments of the English as they stood alone, indomitable, under the Nazi blitzkrieg in the early years of World War II. What seem to the contemporary reader to be embarrassing clichés were, for Boulle, the key to the British character at that time. Also, this was the novel that launched Boulle's writing career, and as such remained his favorite novel despite its evident shortcomings (Interview, 19 November 1990). It is only here that Boulle gives free rein to romantic effusion, untempered by the irony that prevails in the rest of his literary production.

The conversion of William Conrad satisfies our longing for moral rectitude and his heroism conforms to our youthful admiration for the hero, but the actions of the protagonist in *La face* (*Face of a Hero*) give rise to moral ambiguities more reflective of reality than honor and heroic sacrifice. While only three years separate the two novels, the romanticism of *Not the Glory* reflects the state of mind of the young Boulle drawn to Malaya in search of adventure, while the irony and disenchantment of *Face of a Hero* are more in keeping with the sentiments of the patriot whose love of France and liberty led him to imprisonment at the hands of his collaborationist Vichyite countrymen. In neither work, however, does Boulle judge, he merely presents. These are not tracts but novels, and, as a true novelist, Boulle is capable of espousing by turns and with equal conviction the cause of all his characters. As a result, he is able to pardon them whatever their crime may be, demonstrating his belief that the novelist betrays his role of creator if he comments on the action or if he condemns or absolves one or another of his protagonists.

More convincing than the wartime London of *Not the Glory* is the atmosphere in *Face of a Hero* of Boulle's native Provence with its landscape of

> mountains devoid of snow yet eternally crowned with white; mottled hills outlined against the sky like huge leopard skins; battlements of gleaming rock that looked as though some giant had bitten into them; trees rooted

in ocherous shingle that bore no resemblance to trees. . . . torrents cascad-
ing down ravines like those in the New World; villages carved out of sheet
rock clinging to the sides of steep escarpments that were crowned with
medieval castles, flanked by ancient monasteries, riddled with prehistoric
grottoes and surrounded by plains dotted with arenas, triumphal arches,
and Roman aqueducts. He had seen fantastic ruined bridges surmounted
by shrines but leading nowhere: towers, dungeons, and crenelated earth-
works protecting palaces that looked like fortresses. He had driven
through elegant, gloomy towns, followed by towns of another sort: stri-
dent, sprawling towns with shabby, down-at-the-heel inhabitants.[3]

And, above all, there is Boulle's beloved Rhône, unlike any other river,
with its "great width and speed, the strength of its current, and the way
it had of changing in one night from a majestic millpond into a raging
torrent" (*Hero,* 34).

More believable, too, than the stereotypical image of the English gentleman is the firsthand portrait of the Provençal. In this novel, it is precisely the inability of the protagonist to comprehend and to adapt to the
meridional temperament, as well as his efforts to distance himself from
it, that are responsible for the final monstrous miscarriage of justice.
Because Jean Berthier, public prosecutor of the small Provençal town of
Bergerane, is a Northerner, he has exaggerated his native coldness and
reserve without realizing it, not only

> to make his outward appearance conform to the dignity of his position
> but also from some instinctive reaction against a certain slackness in the
> Provençal way of life that rather shocked him on his arrival. Secretly, he
> disapproved of the lackadaisical optimism of the people of Bergerane. He
> was appalled by their openly frivolous behavior and dismayed by their
> singular capacity for being artlessly carried away by the first thing that
> caught their fancy. When he compared this relaxed outlook with the
> industrious, plodding attitude to life of his own people, he could not help
> feeling that he belonged to a different, a stronger and more virile, race.
> This instinctive sense of superiority was reflected not only in his bearing,
> but in his dress as well. (*Hero,* 13)

The basic format of *Face of a Hero* corresponds to that of most of
Boulle's novels in which we find "incidents that are pathetically straightforward in themselves but appalling in their ultimate consequence, that
are clear enough on the surface yet plumb the darkest depths of monstrous improbability, which are as insidious and absurd, as unforgivable
and relentless, as the emotions which at every instant invade a restless

mind" (*Hero,* 10). The "straightforward incident" that triggers the action occurs one Sunday in June when Berthier and his fiancée, Mireille,[4] have picnicked in a secluded cove on the banks of the Rhône. Both have eaten and drunk a little too much and Berthier, throwing discretion to the winds, with a "sweeping gesture of emancipation, almost of revolt . . . had actually taken off his coat before settling down at the foot of the poplar. He had even taken advantage of the blessed solitude of this deserted spot and had rolled up his shirt sleeves. He would never have thought of doing such a thing six months ago, on his arrival in Provence" (*Hero,* 37). Although the conventions of the time may be dated, the bad faith Berthier ultimately demonstrates is sadly timeless.

Mireille is quietly dozing with her head in his lap and Berthier has almost dozed off himself when he hears a strange noise. He looks up and sees a young girl on the other bank of the river, who appears to have had a bicycle accident and is making her way down to the river to wash her cuts and scratches. Berthier, the proper Northerner, is "appalled by the idea of being discovered in his shirt sleeves, lying in the grass with a girl asleep beside him"(*Hero,* 40). Suddenly she stumbles over a loose stone and is unable to hold on because of her injured arm. She falls, striking her head against a rock, and then, losing consciousness, plunges into the river. Berthier does not go to her aid, becoming guilty in effect of negligent homicide.

He vaguely realizes that Mireille's presence is the main reason for his inaction and unpardonable silence. His reason and natural lucidity, and a grotesquely exaggerated sense of his own dignity, make him stop to wonder whether he has enough courage to carry out a dangerous rescue. Were he alone, he would rush to the water's edge and, at the very least, call for help. But Mireille is with him, and he fears to fail in front of her. It is his need for Mireille's admiration, the need to see reflected in her eyes the image he has set up of the incorruptible, perfectly upright human being that governs his actions. His failure to go to the aid of a drowning woman, like that of Clamence, the protagonist of Albert Camus's novel *La chute,* will provoke feelings of guilt; he trembles at the thought of "living forevermore with such a burden of remorse!" (*Hero,* 46).

Despite a certain similarity of circumstances, however, the means by which the two men cope with the problem are very different. Camus's protagonist, always fully cognizant of his culpability, confesses to stimulate others to confess their own sins in order to reassure himself that all men are as much to blame as he; Berthier, on the other hand, seeks to wipe out the memory of his guilt by searching for confirmation of his moral strength in the eyes of others, particularly those of his fiancée. "He leaned over and gazed ardently into her eyes, bitterly rejoicing in the blissful reflection of her faith in him. It was as though he were trying to find the only possible justification for his crime, as though his loathsome cowardice could somehow be excused by her manifestly unchanged confidence" (*Hero*, 47).

The young girl's accidental death is viewed by the police as a homicide. She was seen on the day of her disappearance with Guillaume Vauban, a wealthy wastrel who is frequently violent when he drinks. Witnesses confirm that she had become afraid of him because of his sudden fits of temper and had gone that day to tell him that she could not see him again. They were seen arguing in a café, she left, and he followed soon after. To these facts are added the supposition that Vauban, infuriated by her departure, followed her, attacked her, and threw her body into the river. When her body is found two weeks later, it is covered with bruises consonant with a beating. This body of circumstantial evidence is enough to have the young man indicted for murder. Here Boulle makes an implicit denunciation of capital punishment, for the reader not only knows the true facts behind the young girl's death but also sees how damning circumstantial evidence can be.

Berthier, aware of the truth, cannot speak out because of his inadvertent role in her death. He fears that such an avowal will cause him to forfeit the admiration of the villagers; he sees in their eyes confirmation of his own feelings of superiority and is seized by an irresistible urge to fulfill their hopes by proving that he is the redresser of wrongs they imagine him to be. For he,

> Jean Berthier, was of a different species and came from an altogether different world! He was born in austere surroundings . . . where the climate did not weaken a man's will power, and where compromise did not exist. He came from a long line of virile ancestors, who had devoted their lives to the service of honor and rectitude. . . . It was this absolute conviction of his own superiority that held him in check and prompted him to adopt the only line of conduct compatible with his own dignity. . . . to combat and defeat all these perverse influences so as to deserve the crusader's reputation he had won in the eyes of the people of Bergerane. (*Hero*, 142)

Boulle's portrayal of Berthier makes his terrible act comprehensible. To hide his cowardice from himself, he needs to see reflected in the eyes of others the image he has created of himself as a heroic, upright, highly principled human being. Besides, he resents the efforts made by Vauban's wealthy father to bribe him and the threats to his career when he refuses to drop the case. Here we find another important theme in Boulle's work, the ease with which qualities, in themselves admirable, can yet be misused so that they achieve results that are in direct contradiction to their proper and ostensible purpose. The irony of the situation in *Face of a Hero* lies in the fact that Berthier finds himself calling, in the name of honor and justice, for a condemnation and death penalty that he alone knows to be unwarranted. Yet, in so doing, he is at the same time the champion of the little man, upholding his rights against the forces of privilege, corruption, and unjust influence. Paradoxically, then, honor and justice finally prevail, but at the cost of sending an innocent man to the scaffold.

Boulle has been taxed with the improbability of a man as high-principled and honorable as Berthier being so monstrously callous as to play so prominent a part in a prosecution he knows to be false, yet a person's ability to convince himself of the veracity of something despite all evidence to the contrary, particularly when it absolves him of guilt, is not uncommon. The human capacity for self-delusion, underscored repeatedly in the works of the seventeenth-century moralists, is something that has never failed to fascinate Pierre Boulle; it stands at the center of his work. La Rochefoucauld's maxim, which states, "At times we are as different from ourselves as we are from others,"[5] is echoed by Boulle:

> We abhor any individual who . . . tries to pass himself off as something he is not. The success of such terms as "charlatan" and "fraud" . . . shows the extent of the indignation to which this despicable form of deceit gives rise, and also of the satisfaction we feel on seeing it condemned. . . . A human being who is not all of one piece is still beyond our conception. We refuse to admit that, not fitting into any particular category, he may oscillate perpetually between duplicity and honesty without even being aware of it, and actually exhaust himself in a vain endeavor to reach a state of equilibrium.[6]

Cousin, the protagonist of *Un métier de seigneur* (*A Noble Profession*), embodies this dichotomy. He is an intellectual, who possesses "the supreme qualities of a writer in the most brilliant manner; that is to say, he succeeds with equal felicity in enhancing reality in such a way as to endow it with the glorious hues of artistic fiction and in polishing and marshaling the products of his fantasy in such a rational manner that they eventually assume every appearance of reality" (*Noble*, 12). Cousin prides himself on his own objectivity but actually sees the world through the dreams of his imagined superiority. In September 1939, during the first days of mobilization, he experiences a violent thirst for heroism and sees himself performing outstanding feats of arms, his fantasies nourished by subconscious recollections of stories he had read as a child. During the retreat before the Germans, he is separated from his unit and finds himself alone. As he wanders around aimlessly, he meets Morvan, a French enlisted man who takes him to his home nearby, where they are hidden by Morvan's mother and sister Claire. Cousin convinces Morvan that he is on a secret mission and not merely running away, a rationalization that "had so possessed him that it had lost every trace of fiction" (*Noble*, 25). Boulle once again calls to mind a maxim of La Rochefoucauld, which states: "We cannot get over being deceived by our enemies and betrayed by our friends, yet we are often content to be so treated by ourselves" (La Rochefoucauld, 49). So strong does Cousin's belief in the importance of his putative mission become that he sincerely believes that he—rather than Morvan and Claire, who actually arrange it—is responsible for conceiving and implementing their escape to England in a little boat.

In London, most of the French nationals who wish to carry on the fight are steered into the offices of the Free French. A few, like Morvan and Claire, are given the choice of working directly with the English, he as a radio operator and she as a bilingual stenographer. Cousin is asked to work for the English intelligence service, which permits him to finally realize his schoolboy fantasies of swashbuckling heroism. "Mystery and intrigue add a special pungency to the scent of glory that his mind is forever distilling. 'Intelligence work is a noble profession—an occupation for gentlemen'" (*Noble*, 37).

Accompanied by Morvan as his radio operator, Cousin is sent on a mission to France. He does brilliantly at first, reinforcing his belief in his valor and resourcefulness, but is ultimately captured by the Gestapo. There is a scene of brutal torture, the details of which are left to the reader's imagination. All we learn is that Cousin managed to escape from the Gestapo and has made his way back to England, where he reports that Morvan, fearful of being tortured, had betrayed the secrets of the underground to the Gestapo, only to be killed by them later on. Cousin then volunteers for another mission to France, a surprising move on the part of one who has just escaped death. Dr. Fog, a psychiatrist in charge of recruiting intelligence personnel, notes, however, that those who are so eager to court danger are not absolutely sure of their courage and are frightened that this might be noticed; subconsciously, they are trying to delude themselves and everyone else as well. The doctor's prognosis, like all psychological analysis in Boulle's work, is limited to such superficial pronouncements; the reader never enters into the protagonist's psyche.

Cousin is parachuted into France to make contact with a German traitor who is prepared to sell some information to the Allies. Morvan's sister Claire has volunteered to accompany him on this mission as his radio operator. She has never believed the story of her brother's treason—certain the culprit was in fact Cousin—and is obsessed by the desire to prove his innocence. Cousin knows that Claire is spying on him, waiting for him to make a false move, and forces himself every morning to make a mental effort to revive his favorite fantasies and re-create the image of his ideal hero to gain strength to continue the daily struggle. His torment is increased because he is being blackmailed by the putative German traitor, in reality the head of Nazi intelligence, who is using a tape recording of the torture scene of Cousin's first mission as a weapon to obtain information from him. When Cousin hears the tape,

> a dismal swarm of gruesome memories, which the miraculous will of a mind bent on self-preservation had warded off for several months, now started circling around him . . . drawing nearer and nearer to a certain central image, the axis of their rotation—a human shape none other than himself, bound hand and foot, lying powerless on a heap of straw in a room in a tumble-down farmhouse. When he saw them approaching him with the hot poker, he had cried out in terror: "Stop! stop! I'll talk! I'll tell you everything, everything! I'll do whatever you wish! The whole network . . . the links with London . . . names and addresses, I'll give you the whole thing." (*Noble*, 164–67)

The true story is now revealed. When the Gestapo men brought Cousin back to the room in which the tortured Morvan was lying, Morvan summoned up sufficient strength to lay hold of a submachine gun. Cousin was filled with rage at being torn from his state of numbness, the only condition he found bearable, and especially by Morvan, who, he was sure, only wanted to humiliate him further with this gesture of absurd temerity. If Cousin did not warn the guards, as Nicholson warns the Japanese in *The Bridge over the River Kwai* (see chapter 3), it was only because he was completely paralyzed, deprived of the power of speech by the prospect of violence. After Morvan succeeded in killing the guards, he collapsed in agony. Cousin then worked his way out of his handcuffs, seized the gun, and killed him. "But the elimination of a troublesome witness was not the essential part of his act. The mind makes many other demands! It demands belief in its own virtue. His own mind now demanded that Morvan be the traitor and he, Cousin, a judge created by a divine Providence" (*Noble,* 225).

The fear of being denounced by the German, who poses another threat to the harmonious scenario of his dreams, gives Cousin the courage necessary to kill him. He then proceeds to create a

> revised, improved version of reality, one corresponding so closely to his secret ambition that his mind was unable to question it. Molding, manipulating the raw material of the facts in such a way as to make it yield a satisfactory meaning—that was what he had done all his life. The profession in which he was a past master was now revealed in all its glorious majesty. The exultant sense of his own virtue almost brought tears of enthusiasm to his eyes as he gave the finishing touches to his personality by means of the skillful magic of words. (*Noble,* 232)

Claire, however, manages to overhear part of the tape, which confirms her suspicions. At gunpoint, she confronts Cousin and ties him up, intentionally leaving one of his hands free, and tortures him repeatedly with a hot poker to obtain a confession. Cousin refuses to sign and finally places the cyanide capsule given to each agent in his mouth, breaks the glass with his teeth, and swallows the poison. Why, then, his handler wonders when he receives Claire's report, did Cousin find the courage to undergo torture and then kill himself when he had originally betrayed the Resistance precisely because he was terrified of pain and death? Dr. Fog explains that "the first time it was only a question of the lives of some fifty people. That wasn't a sufficiently clear or striking symbol of duty to enable him to overcome his instincts. Whereas the second time . . . he himself was at stake . . . with that dream world of his—he, the ideal creature of his own imagination! He would have accepted the destruction of everyone on earth . . . but not of that fabulous being. For himself, for himself alone, he was capable of showing heroism" (*Noble,* 251). "Self-love," wrote La Rochefoucauld, "is love of oneself and of all things in terms of oneself; it makes men worshippers of themselves and would make them tyrants over others if fortune gave them the means. It never pauses for rest outside the self and, like bees on flowers, only settles on outside matters in order to draw from them what suits its own requirements" (La Rochefoucauld, 107).

Les vertus de l'enfer (*The Virtues of Hell*), like *A Noble Profession* and *Face of a Hero,* is a masterful dramatization of cowardice, a problem for which it, too, offers a morally ambiguous solution. The protagonist of the novel, John Butler, also the archetypal coward, does not, like Berthier and Cousins, seek to see reflected in the eyes of others a complaisant image that will permit him to continue to believe in his fabricated persona. More like Joseph Conrad's Jim, the protagonist of *Lord Jim,* he is a man engaged in redeeming himself on an absolute plane. But whereas Jim atones for past disgrace and largely vindicates his romantic aspirations, Butler's redemption is due to one overwhelming ambition—the manufacture and delivery of the purest form of heroin in the world. The moral ambiguity at the heart of all of Boulle's work here lies in the fact that Butler is aware that he can rid himself of his addiction to heroin only through the discipline of creative scientific work that will ultimately produce a poison to enslave others. Boulle expresses neither pity nor indignation at this development. He is the dispassionate witness, the "novelist [who] plays the role of a God . . . neither malevolent nor benevolent, but . . . constantly ironic."[7] Boulle here answers to Emile Zola's definition of the experimental novelist as one who works with the absolute objectivity of the scientist to uncover the causes determining human behavior, setting up appropriate experiments that he then carries out with scientific impersonality.

There are, in fact, two scientific experiments in *The Virtues of Hell,* one conducted by the protagonist to manufacture heroin, and one conducted by the author to detoxify his protagonist. A psychiatrist, Dr. Edmund, like Dr. Fog in *A Noble Profession,* plays the role of Greek chorus, appearing from time to time to underscore for the reader the steps in Butler's development from addiction to freedom, from coward to hero. But scientific discipline finally yields here to romantic imagination. Just as Zola's lyric, epic, and visionary genius shaped his novels into something quite different from his so-called experimental novel, Boulle's heroic imagination transforms this work into an old-fashioned action novel, albeit with a flawed hero.

The Virtues of Hell opens in medias res. John Butler, a heroin addict in a desperate state of withdrawal, accosts a solitary pedestrian at gunpoint. Flashbacks reveal the origin of Butler's addiction. Like so many others, he was introduced to heroin in Vietnam, where it helped to dispel the horror of jungle warfare and the memory of its atrocities. Panic stricken when his patrol was ambushed by the Viet Cong, he fled at the first shot, a memory that continues to haunt him and that fuels his addiction. The man he has attempted to rob, who happens to be a drug dealer, gives

Butler money to buy drugs and hires him as a salesman for his large drug-trafficking operation, with the special inducement of a supply of heroin for his personal needs.

Butler's selling skills win the approval of his superiors, who, on the basis of his previous studies in chemistry, offer him a job refining heroin for the operation. Boulle details Butler's course of study as he resumes his education, starting with the general laws of chemistry, progressing to mineral and then organic chemistry, and finally to the transformation of morphine into heroin. Boulle reminds the reader of his scientific background as he explains that "opium contains at least twenty-five different alkaloids, the most important of which is morphine, $C_{17}H_{19}O_3N$ . . . [and that] morphine crystallizes into colorless prisms containing one molecule of water, which it gives up at 212°F."[8] The heroin must then be extracted from the morphine, a process that is simple in theory but difficult in practice, so that the purity of the final product varies considerably according to the chemist's skill. The details about the manufacture of heroin read like a textbook demonstration, as does the story of its distribution.

Butler begins his laboratory work on an Indiana farm. When Treasury agents begin to close in, the operation is moved to a more remote locale—a retreat located on a peak in the rugged Shan States in the Golden Triangle in the north of Burma (Myanmar). He becomes obsessed with the idea of making a purer grade of heroin than ever before achieved; his monomania will transform him completely as it weans him away from his addiction, until he ultimately becomes part of the 10 percent of drug addicts who achieve a permanent cure when they discover the moral support "they needed and were never able to find . . . an outside interest which can take any number of forms. . . . Then gradually they emerge from their mental cocoon, gradually they accustom themselves to the idea of action and become capable of acting. . . . For action and initiative . . . are the criteria for a permanent cure" (*Virtues,* 10–11). The nature and morality of the passion are without importance. Whether money, or gambling, or heroin production, it must be a monomania that takes the place of the drug.

To the consternation of U.S. drug agents, Butler succeeds beyond his wildest expectations. He produces five tons of the purest heroin ever made, but the problem of transporting it to the United States remains. The only feasible plan turns out to be a wild 600-mile trek by mule train southward through the mountains of the Shan States, a formidable obstacle course owing to the rugged terrain of one of the most inaccessible regions on earth, but, for that very reason, unlikely to attract bandits. The journey is to end near the coast at some point along the banks of the Salween, where the goods are to be loaded onto a Chinese junk and taken up the river beyond the densely populated rice-growing sector. It will then go on a junk to Malaya, where it will be hidden in heavy bales of rubber produced on the plantations and, finally, routinely shipped to the West from Penang or Singapore.[9]

Butler, uncharacteristically, asks to join the expedition, troubled by the idea of the dangerous journey that awaits the treasure he has so patiently amassed. He is euphoric when he receives approval to accompany the expedition. It is here that the romantic adventures begin. Following in the tradition of the hero, Butler takes an increasingly active role, unchallenged by the others, and becomes the de facto leader of the expedition when he routs the Lahu tribesmen who ambush the mule train and succeeds in saving most of the shipment. His men now treat him with great respect and are prepared to follow him anywhere.

The legend of Butler, the former failure, coward, and drug addict, begins to take shape, spreading from Burma to Thailand. In the course of his transformation, he has become not only a heroic figure but also a great, compassionate leader. In a scene reminiscent of the final scene in Malraux's *La condition humaine,* where Katow gives his cyanide capsules to two of his comrades to spare them the torture of being burned alive in the boiler of a locomotive, Butler gives 8 of the 10 doses of heroin he has put aside for his own needs during the journey to his wounded men. When asked about his incredible action, he replies that he no longer requires drugs, that without realizing it he has been detoxified. He needs nothing but the glory of his achievement: "He had brought the expedition through safely—a trek unprecedented in the narcotic traffic annals and which promised to become as legendary as his record in the laboratory" (*Virtues,* 189).

The shipment finally reaches its destination in the United States, to which it has been tracked by the Drug Enforcement Agency. Butler's apotheosis is complete when, surrounded by U.S. agents who plan to seize the heroin, he refuses to surrender, he "the hero of the Shan States, whose name was idolized in every mountain hut . . . this gallant knight . . . was not about to throw down his sword and give himself up!"(*Virtues,* 204–5). He sets fire to the delivery trucks to prevent the heroin from falling into the hands of the drug agents and finally dies heroically, "on the battlements" one might be tempted to read, defending—not liberty, not justice, not the oppressed, not even financial interest—nothing but a shipment of heroin for which he has already been paid. But, paradoxically, it is this heroin, his creation, that has given meaning to his life and a cause for which to die.

Pierre Boulle's characters for the most part appear at the outset to be average people; they have normal occupations and seem destined to lead ordinary lives. But there is something in their nature that forces them to push themselves to the limit; they are enslaved by an idée fixe whose coercive power transforms them and drives them inexorably towards a grotesque destiny. In the case of the photographer Martial Gaur, the protagonist of *Le photographe* (*The Photographer*), it is the single-minded pursuit of the perfect picture—the exceptional document that has always eluded him—that is the instrument for this dehumanization. A critic has remarked that *The Photographer* is built on a conflict between the personal and professional personalities of the protagonist,[10] ignoring the fact that Boulle's characters possess neither a public nor a private personality. Prisoners of a single passion, they are nothing but puppets controlled by their monomania.

Gaur, once an outstanding war photographer, had played the role of impartial observer in every conflict, "with the same equally divided contempt for beliefs, opinions and parties, the same ethical indifference to ignoble acts and meritorious acts, feats of valor and feats of cowardice, only working himself up into a state of enthusiasm, but then to the highest degree, when human passions revealed themselves through outstanding images which were sufficiently evocative and unusual to justify a photograph."[11] He has had to content himself with still pictures of movie starlets since he lost one of his legs in Algeria. Handicapped now by an artificial leg, he can no longer go in search of action, and can only occasionally photograph exceptional events thanks to one of his friends, the chief bodyguard of the president of the Republic.

The bodyguard's job is particularly difficult at the moment because the new president is a controversial figure, hated by the traditional right-wing parties because of his liberal reforms and his impending marriage to a beautiful actress half his age. Coincidentally, just before the president's marriage, Olga, a young woman of unnatural intensity, moves into Gaur's hotel and into his bed. Gaur discovers by chance that she is part of a plot to assassinate the president and is using him to obtain information about the movements of the chief of state. He decides to turn the tables and use her instead in his pursuit of the one shot in a million.

Gaur is now ready for the great destiny that awaits him as he orchestrates the assassination of the president, as if he were God. In conformity with the rules of his profession, which stipulate that the photographer must visualize in advance the general construction of his picture, he must not merely record but must also create. It is as necessary for the photographer as for the painter to transpose and transcend reality, leaving his imprint on even the most transitory image. The fact that he is arranging a murder is of no importance, for "the photographer is an artist [and] . . . the artist must be capable of being inhuman" (*Photographer,* 98).

Weaving a web of delicate intrigue, Gaur waits for the moment he wants to immortalize on film. "He sees himself as a sort of demiurge commanding a confused chaos of elements and directing them towards a creation whose advent no one but himself could foresee" (*Photographer,* 113). Feigning naïveté, he informs the assassins about the president's movements and makes it possible for them to murder him, as he takes exceptional photographs of the assassination with the unthinking cruelty of the child who watches an animal die. Just as the point of the knife pierces the president's chest, Gaur presses the shutter release for the first time. "The expression of hatred engraved at this moment on Olga's face would of itself have justified the value of this picture. He still had time to take a second exposure . . . a point blank view of the wretched President, now mortally wounded, a photograph which fixed for eternity all the horror of the death agony, enhanced by a profusion of details which no photographer had ever before assembled in one exposure, a unique document by virtue of the personality of the subject . . . [and] the sumptuousness of the setting" (*Photographer,* 174–75).

The Photographer is not a novel of manners or morals; the plot and characters are also unimportant. They are merely a pretext for a development as rigorous as a mathematical proposition. For Boulle, the true story, the only story, is not that of morality, emotions, descriptions, or events but the individual adventure of the protagonist and the logical sequence of actions called forth by his monomania. Verisimilitude is so unimportant that the novel stops short at the moment at which Gaur realizes his goal.

The power of irresistible desires reappears at the center of *Pour l'amour de l'art* (For art's sake),[12] a novel constructed in the form of a medieval "sotie," or moralizing farce. With characteristic irony, Boulle here deflates the pretentious egos of ambitious magistrates, screen stars, demagogic politicians and their sycophants as he details the excesses engendered by blind adherence to a fabricated image. Irresistible dreams transform the main characters completely as each of them seeks in his interaction with the others that which he has lost in the exercise of his official responsibilities.

Néron, the surname of the president of the Republic, which calls to mind the evil Roman emperor, might lead the reader to posit evil behind the president's clandestine weekly meetings with a companion in the apartment of his confidential secretary. But this, it soon appears, is not the case. The president is closeted with a famous actor, Claude Baudinard, to learn how to conduct himself best before the television cameras. The lessons have been arranged by a distinguished former actress named Clara. Now an impresario, Clara is obsessed by the realization of a superproduction that, like Gaur's photograph, will be the ultimate triumph of her career.

During the course of their lessons, the student/president and the professor/actor make two parallel discoveries: Néron realizes that the form of the speech makes a greater impact on the audience than its content, and Baudinaud discovers the fascination of ideas. The logical consequence of this is that the two men change professions; Baudinaud becomes president and Néron, taken in hand by Clara, becomes Z., the incomparable star of the great theatrical work she is preparing. One understands the actor who is attracted to the political arena, knowing that actors have, indeed, become presidents.[13] We have also seen presidents who cannot resist the excitement of the theater, performing in public on the piano or saxophone as if they were entertainers. Thus, we need not suspend disbelief here. What is impossible to accept, however, is a subplot—an unusual occurrence in Boulle's work—centered around a barrister who delays the arrest of a serial child murderer, permitting another murder to be committed. The barrister does this so that he can relive his glories as a trial lawyer by taking on the murderer's seemingly hopeless case. To expand what would otherwise be an amusing short story into a novel, Boulle introduces this preposterous character, uncharacteristically complicating the plot and transforming a clever conceit into a pedestrian work.

The life of Emperor Frederick II, king of Germany and Sicily, last of the great Hohenstaufen rulers, crowned Holy Roman emperor in 1220—*L'étrange croisade de l'empereur Frédéric II* (The strange crusade of Emperor Frederick II)—illustrates what Pierre Boulle believes to be one of the great ironies of life, the contradictions that exist between reason and action. The urge to do what we must not do is, according to Boulle, one of the most powerful human drives. Indeed, the acts of certain people can be attributed to an unusual force that pushes them instinctively, or perhaps for reasons known only to themselves, to defy all expectations and act in an unpredictable manner on certain important occasions. This subtle art, which is impossible to analyze, Boulle calls "the art of disconcerting,"[14] one at which Frederick II excelled and which places him squarely within the family of the author's fictional heroes.

Frederick had ties to almost all of Europe through his family, his inheritance, and his titles. His cosmopolitanism was also fostered by the disruption of existing economic boundaries that occurred at the beginning of the thirteenth century, owing largely to the fact that the Crusades were transformed from the religious expeditions of the past into commercial endeavors stimulated by a desire to reconquer the commercially valuable sea routes of the Mediterranean. This change in the true purpose of the Crusades was also of great interest to the popes, who saw in the reconquest of the Mediterranean the possibility of a rebirth of the former political and economic importance of Rome.

Frederick was 10 years old when he heard about the crusaders who turned away from the Holy Land to conquer and sack the wealthy city of Constantinople. This probably explains why years later, on the day of his coronation as king of Germany at Aix-la-Chapelle, he grasped the crucifix and swore to embark on a crusade to free the Holy Places—a crusade he deferred for 12 years. Ironically, when he finally left on his holy expedition, he had been excommunicated, ostensibly for impiety and debauchery but actually because the pope feared his growing power. It was only when the crusade was forbidden to him by the Church that Frederick began to prepare it in earnest. The 12 intervening years had given him time in which to organize a mission to suit his purposes without recourse to a regular army. Although there were a few hundred soldiers on his boats for unforeseen emergencies, the main body of the mission consisted primarily of philosophers, mathematicians, naturalists, and other experts to study in situ astrology, astronomy, chemistry, alchemy, agriculture, and medicine. There were also singers, musicians, dancers, and even many Muslims who were born in his kingdom of Sicily. Frederick's crusade was carried out with the most complete religious indifference. It was in fact "an avant-garde detachment of the old slumbering western world, awakened by a prince who anticipated the Renaissance by two centuries as he searched for enlightenment by shaking off the dust of the Middle Ages" (*Frédéric,* 134). What the imperial galleys carried on this day of 28 June 1228 "was not a army of ferocious warriors, of fanatics determined to engage in battle, it was a carefully prepared cultural, scientific, and artistic mission that Frederick was

taking toward the mysterious Orient to learn about its superior civilization and bring back to the West valuable knowledge" (*Frédéric*, 138).

Frederick succeeded in retaking Jerusalem by diplomatic means and
virtually without bloodshed, whereas a little more than a century before
the devout crusaders had massacred in the space of only two days 40,000
people, mostly defenseless citizens. Notwithstanding his success, his
excommunication was not rescinded, almost as if the pope held his triumph against him. Later, back in favor, Frederick lived like an Oriental
potentate at his court in Sicily, surrounded by scholars, by members of
all religions and cultures, and by a harem and its eunuchs.

The paradoxes of Frederick's career delighted the skeptic Boulle.
Boulle highlights, just as Voltaire did in *Candide,* the incongruities of an
emir transformed by Frederick into a Christian knight, of Muslim
troops used by the crusading emperor against the papal troops, and of
the elegant gentlemen's agreement with the Sultan Al Camil, which
permitted Frederick to free the Holy Places, reestablish freedom of religion, and ensure peaceful and tolerant coexistence to both Christians
and Muslims. For Boulle, Frederick is a character in search of a stage, an
actor required by History to write his own part. Action for him was a
form of provocation. In a world in which passion rather than circum-
spection ruled, Frederick symbolized intellectual curiosity, so much so
that, in an experiment that calls to mind several outrageous demonstrations performed by Boulle in his science fiction stories,[15] Frederick
locked a condemned man in a barrel to see whether his soul would fly
away at the moment of death.

Whether they live seven centuries in the past, as in *L'étrange croisade
de l'empéreur Frédéric II,* in the twentieth century, or seven centuries in the
future, as in his works of science fiction, whether they live in Europe or
in Southeast Asia, on Earth or on a remote planet, all of Boulle's protagonists belong to the same family, united by their infinite capacity for self-
delusion and their monomaniacal pursuit of a chosen goal. The universe
in which they move is amoral—Boulle does not judge, he just transcribes
what he sees. He is a moralist in the seventeenth-century sense of the
word, one who observes human behavior and who notes his observations
most often in the form of fables and maxims.

Chapter Three
Southeast Asia

Pierre Boulle's experiences in Southeast Asia provided invaluable background material for several of his novels, but his attraction to the absurd or strange is innate, he maintains, and does not reflect the influence of the Orient. The plots and a large number of the characters in these novels, other than the autobiographical novel *S.O.P.H.I.A.*, are invented; only the scenery and atmosphere are completely authentic (Interview, 28 November 1992). The best known of these novels, and undoubtedly the most outstanding in all of Boulle's oeuvre, is *The Bridge over the River Kwai*, which was awarded the Prix Sainte-Beuve in 1952. In this, Boulle's third novel, all of the elements of his literary art converge against the background of Southeast Asia. Boulle's mastery of the storyteller's art is nowhere more apparent than in this remarkable novel where we find, together with certain autobiographical elements, variations on several of the author's most important themes—among them the transformation of a man under the pressure of circumstances, the inevitable corruption of all human enterprise, and the relativity between good and evil. Evident, too, in this novel is Boulle's insistence on painting men as they are, not as they should be.

The resemblance of the protagonist of Boulle's famous novel *The Bridge over the River Kwai* to those of his other works is emphasized from the very beginning by the epigraph, which is taken from Joseph Conrad's *Victory:* "No, it was not funny: it was rather pathetic; he was so representative of all the past victims of the Great Joke. But it is by folly alone that the world moves, so it is a respectable thing upon the whole. And, besides, he was what one would call a good man" (*Kwai*, 5). Similarly, here, as in his other novels, Boulle refuses to pronounce judgment. To those who saw it as a thesis novel directed against war, Boulle countered: "As far as I am concerned, my novel is neither militaristic nor anti-militaristic, nor for that matter is it 'istic' in any other way. . . . I intended it to be the illustration of a general 'absurdity' which could as well have been located in other times, other places and with other personages."[1] Boulle's concept of absurdity differs from that of the existentialists, who posit an irreconcilable divorce between man and the universe, between the human longing for meaning and order and the meaninglessness and disorder of existence. For Boulle, absurdity results from the "lack of congruity between the motives explaining a certain conduct and the results achieved when one follows to the letter the 'good' principles motivating this particular behavior" (Joyaux, 179). The absurdity of virtue shading into vice, of duty and honor leading to betrayal, is at the heart of *The Bridge over the River Kwai.*

The action of the novel takes place in 1942 during the first months of World War II in the Pacific theater, when the Japanese forces, carried along by the momentum of their victories, were organizing the conquered territories and preparing new conquests. The occupation of French Indochina and then of Siam (Thailand) had opened the road to Malaya, which the Japanese invaded soon after the bombing of Pearl Harbor on 7 December 1941. Two months later, the surrender of the British naval base at Singapore permitted the Japanese to concentrate on plans for the invasion of India. Once their armies started driving toward India, the Japanese needed a railway line across Siam and Burma (Myanmar) and they forced prisoners of war from the dozens of labor camps along the Kwai River to construct it. Although Boulle knew the general area, and although he took the river's real name, he made no pretense to literal authenticity in his novel. "I didn't know the River Kwai when I wrote the book. I took an atlas and I looked for a river where they were building the Siam-Burma Railway for the purpose of invading India. Eighty thousand English prisoners lost their lives building that railroad."[2] The bridge that the British prisoners of war constructed over the River Kwai at Tha Makham, some 80 miles west of Bangkok, was not the fictional bridge that Boulle placed near the Burma frontier, 200 miles from the only actual bridge across the Kwai.[3]

The protagonist of *The Bridge over the River Kwai,* Colonel Nicholson, is the commander of British troops in a prisoner-of-war camp. Nicholson, a living example of the Indian Army officer made famous in the writings of Kipling, exhibits the archetypal "sense of duty, observance of ritual, obsession with discipline, and love of the job well done" (*Kwai,* 12). In the past, Nicholson's high regard for discipline had been a byword in various parts of Asia and Africa. In 1942 it was once again in evidence at Singapore during the disaster that followed the invasion of Malaya. When orders came to surrender, he dissuaded a group of young officers from escaping. "Since the commander in chief had signed the surrender for the whole of Malaya," he reasoned, "not one of His Majesty's subjects could escape without committing an act of disobedience" (*Kwai,* 12). Boulle, as he explains in *My Own River Kwai,* was undoubtedly influenced in his portrayal of Nicholson by the conduct of Vichyite officers and civil servants who let themselves be caught in a de facto betrayal of France as a result of too strict an attachment to the rules of military discipline.

It is in keeping with his military sense of honor and discipline that Nicholson refuses to permit his officers to perform manual labor on the bridge when the drunken, sadistic Japanese camp commander, Colonel Saito, in clear violation of the code of military conduct of the Hague Convention, orders them to do so. Saito is a caricature meant to heighten the contrast between Japanese barbarous brutality and English civilized behavior, a theme that runs throughout the book. In his portrayal of British courage in adversity and the technological superiority of the Western over the Oriental mind, Boulle here continues his wartime love affair with the indomitable England that rejected France's disgraceful surrender and collaboration.

Nicholson resists Saito's torture so bravely that he eventually succeeds in carrying his point; the officers are to be exempt from manual labor. After his victory over the Japanese commander, Nicholson decides to build an incomparably better bridge than the one the Japanese would have built, in order to re-establish the morale of his troops and vindicate his own patriotic pride. The bridge is to be a masterpiece, one that will reinforce the colonial myth of the superiority of western organized efficiency to Japanese technological ineptitude. The irony here, of which Boulle is quite aware and in which he delights, is that, in truth, the Japanese had just beaten the Allies in a campaign that showed their remarkable command of very difficult engineering and transport problems. They were perfectly capable of building their own bridges.

Saito realizes he will never complete the bridge unless he permits the British to handle it in their own way. Paradoxically, what happens then is a form of collaboration. For their own self-respect, one of the keys to survival, the prisoners are compelled by Nicholson to make a good job of the bridge, and the success is such that in the end the colonel himself regards it not merely as a morale builder but also as a lasting memorial to the suffering and skill of his men in impossible circumstances. Ian Watt, a lieutenant in the British army during World War II and one of the tens of thousands of Allied prisoners of war who slaved for the Japanese on the Burma-Siam railway, writes that there was some basis in fact for such collaboration. His own commander had initially refused repeated demands that all officer prisoners of war be sent out to build the railway until they were all ordered on parade one morning. When the Japanese guards took up their positions and loaded their rifles and machine guns, the British colonel in charge felt obliged to yield. Officers soon started doing manual labor on the railway in every camp where there were more of them than were absolutely needed to administer the troops.[4] Watt adds that they had not been able to avoid going rather far in collaborating with the Japanese. To survive they had actively helped the enemy by playing an important supervisory role in the building of a strategic military railway. Even so, whatever they were forced to do, their collaboration had not gone nearly as far as in Boulle's novel.

It was certainly pure fantasy for Boulle to write of dying men leaving the hospital hut and "going to work with a smile on their lips" (*Kwai,* 146), just out of devotion to their colonel. In truth, according to Watt, the men had performed at the point of Japanese bayonets and certainly not to please a colonel. Respect for superior rank had weakened considerably under prison conditions, and any colonel who acted the way Nicholson had would have been replaced, as had been the case with many incompetent or unbalanced commanding officers (Watt 1959, 86). The blind obedience once seen at the massacres at Gallipoli and during the infamous charge of the Light Brigade, for example, was a thing of the past, and Nicholson would not have survived in a real prison camp. Still, there was something in the point made by Boulle, since Nicholson's monomaniacal commitment to the bridge was essentially a desperate effort to permit him and his men to share the solidarity that comes from "concentrating on something that would last" (*Kwai,* 219).

The construction of a perfect bridge becomes Nicholson's obsession. For him, as for Boulle's other monomaniacs, action shapes and governs thought. "He witnessed this gradual materialization [of the bridge] without connecting it in any way with humble human activity. Consequently, he saw it only as something abstract and complete in itself: a living symbol of the fierce struggles and countless experiments by which a nation gradually raises itself in the course of centuries to a state of civilization" (*Kwai,* 109–10). His obsession, a form of madness to which the reader of Boulle's fiction is accustomed, infects two subordinates, Major Hughes and Captain Reeves. They become as blind as their leader as they, too, let their passions override their intellect.

Still, it is important to note that the construction of the bridge offered them an opportunity to create something of beauty and value, unhampered by tradition-bound administrations, budget limitations, or fear of innovation. For Captain Reeves, in particular, in peacetime a public-works engineer in India, the bridge was the chance he had been waiting for all his life. "He had always dreamed of tackling a really big job without being badgered every other minute by administrative departments or maddened by interfering officials who ask ridiculous questions and try to put a spoke in the wheels on the pretext of economy, thereby frustrating every creative attempt. Here he was responsible to the Colonel and to no one else" (*Kwai*, 90). Then, too, in the power struggle between the prisoner and his jailer, there is a need to demonstrate that, in spite of the appearances of subjugation and loss of liberty, the prisoner can establish his own superiority, even if that superiority is reduced to the confines of his own mind.

Initially, the struggle is between the British and their Japanese captors. There are, however, three free Englishmen, introduced in the second part of the novel, members of Commando Force 316[5] whose mission is to blow up the bridge. The struggle in the rest of the novel is no longer between East and West; it is now between two Western groups, one committed to building the bridge and the other to destroying it. And, at the center of the novel, serving as a link between both parts, is the bridge, a product of the imagination of a man whose fascination with bridges can be traced back to his youth in Avignon, site of the legendary ruined bridge celebrated in the folk song "Sur le pont d'Avignon."

In the preface to the 1963 edition of *The Bridge over the River Kwai*, Boulle writes:

> When I was of university age, I dreamed of building bridges, and I studied with passion the principles of static pressure and the strength of materials. A little later, during the war, I learned how to destroy bridges, and that prospect filled me with an excitement comparable to that of young Joyce in this story. I never had the opportunity, alas, either to build or to destroy a bridge, and that has remained one of the regrets of my life. Then, when peace was restored, I set about to think up and to tell the story of a bridge, and I threw myself into this new adventure with as much enthusiasm as at the time of my technical studies. . . . After years of reflection, I am incapable of determining which of these enterprises was more sound. . . . Perhaps they are both equivalent; perhaps the result is of only limited importance; perhaps the value of an act lies only in the passion one brings to it?[6]

The action of the novel shifts back and forth between the construction of the bridge and the preparations for its destruction. The headquarters of Force 316, nicknamed The Plastic and Destructions Co., Ltd. (*Kwai*, 61), is located in Calcutta and is commanded by Colonel Green, who is responsible for planning operations. He receives information that operations on the Burma-Siam railway are progressing and that, despite the ghastly conditions and appalling losses of men, the task will be completed in a few months. Colonel Green decides to send a demolition team into the railway area and recruits three British officers for the mission. The leader of the team, Major Shears, an excavalry officer and one of Force 316's founding members, is to get in touch with the Siamese (Thais), make sure of their good intentions and loyalty, and then start training the partisans. The second officer, Captain Warden, a former professor of Oriental languages, speaks Siamese, and the third, Joyce, an industrial engineer in civilian life and Boulle's alter ego, is the demolitions expert. Joyce's engineering background, his commando training in Calcutta, his experiences in the jungle, and his raft journey down the River Kwai are based on Boulle's experiences (see chapter 1); only his adventures and his fate are different.

The bridge is virtually finished; all that remains now is what the colonel calls the " 'trimmings,' which will give the construction that 'finished' look in which the practical eye can at once recognize, in no matter what part of the world, the craftsmanship of the European and the Anglo-Saxon sense of perfection" (*Kwai,* 146). It is at this moment that those bent on destroying this "perfection," the members of Force 316, arrive on the scene. The demolition team is to wait until the entire railway is finished and deliver a single, powerful blow rather than risk giving the whole show away by a series of minor attacks. Warden reaches an observation post on the opposite side of the river from the labor camp, while Shears, Joyce, and two Siamese volunteers, accompanied by a few porters, set off downstream on a raft to set the charges, attaching them to the piles of the bridge. The detonators are inserted at the same time as the charges are fixed, and they are then linked together with a network of "instantaneous" fuses, so that all the explosions occur simultaneously. They swim to shore carrying the battery and playing out the wire, which they camouflage in the undergrowth. Then Shears rejoins Warden to cover the withdrawal after the explosion, and, after setting up the battery and generator, Joyce remains in hiding on the enemy bank to wait for the train the following morning. Yet, as Boulle learned from his own ill-fated raft trip—a theme that recurs throughout his work—"an operation never takes place according to plan. At the last moment there is always some small, trivial, sometimes grotesque occurrence which upsets the most carefully worked-out program" (*Kwai,* 184). And so it is here; the water receded during the night and the electric wire is now visible. Shears sees this from above and Joyce, alone in his hideout, notices the electric wire lying exposed on the beach. He takes hold of his knife and waits to see what will happen. Just then Nicholson starts to cross the bridge.

> With a clear conscience, at peace with the universe and with God, gazing through eyes that were bluer than the tropical sky after a storm, feeling through every pore of his ruddy skin the satisfaction of the well-earned rest that is due to any craftsman after a difficult task, proud of having overcome every obstacle through his personal courage and perseverance, glorying in the work accomplished by himself and by his men in this corner of Siam which he now felt almost belonged to him, light at heart at the thought of having shown himself worthy of his forefathers and of having contributed a far from common chapter to the Eastern legends of empire-builders, firmly convinced that no one could have done the job better, confirmed in his certainty of the superiority of his own race in every field of activity . . . delighted with the quality of the construction, anxious to see for himself, and for the last time, the sum total of its perfection compounded of hard work and intelligence, and also in order to carry out a final inspection, Colonel Nicholson strode with dignity across the bridge over the River Kwai. (*Kwai*, 204)

Nicholson notices the charges, now visible on the piles of the bridge, calls to Saito, and then goes down to the beach where he sees the wire. Warden is startled to see that it is Nicholson who is leading the Japanese to the wire, crying out to Colonel Saito that the bridge has been mined. At the same time, Joyce creeps up from behind and cuts the Japanese colonel's throat. He identifies himself to Nicholson as a British officer and warns him that the bridge is to be blown up. Driven into a frenzy at the thought that his achievement and that of his men may soon be destroyed, Nicholson follows Joyce up to the generator and falls on him, preventing him from throwing the switch. He then cries out to the Japanese for help. Shears jumps into the water and swims toward the enemy bank, where he is struck down by the Japanese soldiers who have come to the beach on hearing Nicholson's cries. Shears collapses alongside of the unconscious Joyce, and the Japanese cut the wire from the detonator. While the train manages to pass safely over the bridge, it is blown up by a fog signal that had been laid just below the observation post on the far side of the bridge. The engine jumps the track and plunges into the water, bringing two or three coaches down with it. Although a few of the enemy are drowned and a fair amount of stores lost, the bridge remains intact. To make sure that Joyce and Shears will not be tortured by their captors, Warden gives the order to fire, killing them, Colonel Nicholson, and several Japanese soldiers. Boulle tells us that he wrote this final scene first; the rest was written to lead up to it.

On his return to base in Calcutta, Warden, the only survivor of the trio, remarks ironically to Colonel Green:

> More insight, that's what he [Joyce] needed; then he would have known who his enemy really was, realized it was that old blockhead who couldn't stand the idea of his fine work being destroyed. . . . That old brute with his blue eyes had probably spent his whole life dreaming of constructing something which would last. In the absence of a town or a cathedral, he plumped for this bridge. You couldn't really expect him to let it be destroyed—not a regular of the old school, sir, not likely! I'm sure he had read the whole of Kipling as a boy, and I bet he recited chunks of it as the construction gradually took shape above the water. "Yours is the Earth and everything that's in it, And—which is more—you'll be a Man, my son!" (*Kwai,* 219)[7]

Nicholson's descent into madness is evidence of Boulle's repudiation of the concept of "the white man's burden." Despite the portrayal of the Japanese as barbarians, Boulle balances the scales by showing the futility of Western expertise with its equal commitment to construction and destruction. For rather than a colonialist, Boulle is a guide to the colonial mentality. Indeed, rather than the work of Kipling, this novel calls to mind Voltaire's *contes philosophiques.* Even more telling are the reflections of the medical officer, Major Clipton, which open the novel:

> The insuperable gap between East and West that exists in some eyes is perhaps nothing more than an optical illusion. Perhaps it is only the conventional way of expressing a popular opinion based on insufficient evidence and masquerading as a universally recognized statement of fact, for which there is no justification at all, not even the plea that it contains an element of truth. During the war, "saving face" was perhaps as vitally important to the British as it was to the Japanese. . . . Perhaps the mentality of the Japanese colonel, Saito, was essentially the same as that of his prisoner, Colonel Nicholson. (*Kwai,* 9–10)

All of the philosophical implications and complexities of the novel are lost, unfortunately, in the translation from novel to film. In spite of the fact that *The Bridge over the River Kwai* was first published in 1952, it was not until 1957, when the American Sam Spiegel produced and Sir David

Lean directed the film *The Bridge on the River Kwai*—which won seven Academy Awards—that the novel received worldwide notice.[8] The plot of the film, at least in outline, follows the novel quite closely, yet changes were made that undercut the presentation of Boulle's ideas and transformed the film into a visually spectacular and exciting adventure story with a stunning jungle setting.

The most significant of the changes was the casting of American film star William Holden as the protagonist of the film, rather than the English actor Alec Guinness, who plays Colonel Nicholson. The British commando Shears, a secondary character in the novel, is now an American prisoner of war played by Holden, whose role is built around the actor's familiar screen persona—the shallow, handsome, good-for-nothing ladies' man. The cynical American antihero is unconvincing at first in his criticism of Nicholson's blind belief in military duty and honor in the name of "living like a human being," when he has been shown by his words and actions to be devoid of the most elementary notions of responsibility or morality. It is only when we see the increasing folly of Nicholson that we are encouraged to reconsider Shears's cynicism and credit his viewpoint.[9]

Holden-Shears—hyphenated here because the character in Boulle's novel is appropriated by the actor—is a prisoner in the camp when Nicholson and his men arrive. He is already plotting his escape, which he effects shortly afterward. There follows an exciting cinematographic chase scene in which his two companions are killed. Holden-Shears, himself, is shot, falls into the river, crawls through the jungle pursued by vultures, and collapses in a friendly jungle village, where he is nursed back to health.[10] The Siamese natives in the film support the Europeans and yearn to free their country from the Japanese, a myth Boulle refutes both in *S.O.P.H.I.A.* and in *The Test,* where he shows that the supreme desire of all colonized people is to be rid of foreigners in order to pursue their lives without outside interference.

Dressed in leis and a red-checked sarong, Holden-Shears secures a small boat with the help of the villagers and sets out for the sea. Then follows the obligatory adventure scene in which the hero floats for days under the tropical sun, uses up all of his water, becomes delirious, drinks the polluted river water, and lies dying in the bottom of the boat. The visual excitement generated by this and other such encounters with death in the film are more suited to that medium than the unheroic, unphotogenic deaths described by Boulle in the novel, where the men die of starvation, malaria, dysentery, gangrene, jungle fever, beriberi, snake bites, and bullet wounds. The film does not show us the skeletons who were "nothing but skin and bone, covered with ulcers and jungle sores" (*Kwai,* 134).

Holden-Shears reappears at a hospital in Ceylon (Sri Lanka), where he is recovering after having been rescued off camera by a British seaplane. He is summoned to the office of Major Warden, director of Force 316, who informs him that they have discovered the existence of the bridge over the River Kwai and that they are going in to bomb it. They need him to serve as a guide because of his familiarity with the precise location of the camp and the bridge. He refuses at first, and the viewer, who has seen the folly of Nicholson's obsessive idea of commitment, duty, and self-sacrifice, seconds him in his rejection of blind obedience and devotion to duty. He is forced to "volunteer," since the authorities have discovered that he is actually an enlisted man masquerading as an officer and threaten him with court-martial and execution.

The former prisoner of war Holden-Shears, now a commando, is used to unify the two separate parts of the plot. The action scene showing the parachute jump made by the commandos into Siam, another cinematic convention, adds spectacle and excitement to the film; but the requisite sex scenes, another cliché of the genre, are disconcerting intrusions into the novel's male universe of prison camps and commando raids. The first of them, Holden-Shears's affair with a blond nurse at the hospital in Ceylon, is a standard box-office ingredient. Still, when four "luscious" Siamese girls leave their jungle village to serve as bearers for the commandos, the film deteriorates into a tropical fantasy. "What's a nice girl like you doing in a place like this?" Holden-Shears asks one of the bearers, to the viewer's dismay. In another scene, just before the descent on the raft to mine the bridge, the two prettiest of the bearers smear camouflage paint on the commandos with lingering caresses.

While the character of Holden-Shears was created out of whole cloth for the film, Nicholson and Saito bear considerable resemblance to their fictional counterparts. Nevertheless, certain changes in the makeup of the two men distort the basic ideas in Boulle's novel. The Japanese commandant of the film is a frustrated artist and a man articulate about his pride rather than the cruel, sadistic, incompetent drunkard of Boulle's novel. The ultimate cliché in the film is the scene in which Saito prepares to expiate his shame at being bested by Nicholson by committing hara-kiri, "just like all the proud Samurai warriors in the movies and just unlike all the hundreds of real Japanese officers who were concerned with prisoners of war" (Watt 1959, 92).

Although Nicholson no longer occupies center stage in the film, he is in most respects identical to the character in the novel. Still, the few changes that were made in the film significantly alter Boulle's intentions. Boulle's monomaniacs require no external stimuli to foster their obsessions, but Nicholson's madness in the film can be traced in part to his ordeal in solitary confinement. Further, Boulle never explains the psychology of his characters: "I try to find acts," he remarks, "behavior that conveys the thoughts of the characters. That is the most important quality in a novelist. I don't like long speeches. And the psychology of the character should become apparent from his behavior. It seems to me that I followed that line of conduct in almost all of my novels" (Interview, 19 November 1992).

Uncharacteristically, Nicholson becomes introspective in the film, as he admires the beauty of the bridge in one of the final scenes and explains his obsession with it to Saito: "I've been thinking. Tomorrow it will be twenty-eight years to the day that I have been in the service, in peace and war. . . . Still, it's been a good life. I love India, I wouldn't have had it any other way, but there are times when suddenly you realize you are nearer the end than the beginning. You wonder, you ask yourself what the sum total of your life represents, what difference your being there made—or if it made any difference at all—really, particularly in comparison with other men's careers. . . . But tonight, tonight."

Nicholson's confession paves the way for his conversion in the final scene, a thrilling spectacle that, unfortunately, thoroughly alters Boulle's thematic intentions. In the film as in the novel, Joyce falls upon Saito and slits his throat. He is then thrown to the ground by Nicholson, as Holden-Shears swims over to help him. In the film, however, Nicholson recognizes Holden-Shears and, at the same time, realizes his error. "What have I done?," he cries out, as, wounded by one of Warden's mortar shells, he collapses on top of the detonator plunger, thereby blowing up the bridge. Boulle disapproved of this dénouement. "In my book," he states, "the bridge is not blown up, the colonel remains faithful to his ideal, he saves his bridge. I do not agree with the movie's end" (Interview, 19 November 1990). Although Nicholson's change of heart and the blowing up of the bridge are in keeping with the conventions of Hollywood, which insist that evil be punished and that "our side" triumph in the end, the paradoxes and absurdities of life at the center of Boulle's oeuvre are eliminated and good and reason prevail.

When *The Bridge over the River Kwai* was first published, the consensus was that it was unbelievable. When the film was produced, however, everyone believed that it was a true story. It was also the film, according to Watt, that created the "myth" of the River Kwai. "The decisive phase of a myth," he remarks "is when the story wins a special status for itself; people think of it, not exactly as history, but as an action which, in some vague way, really happened: and eventually the fiction imposes itself on the world as literally true. The earliest signs of this are normally the erection of shrines, and the beginning of pilgrimages; but the process of reincarnation is only complete when whatever is left of the truth which conflicts with the myth's symbolic meaning is forgotten or transformed. All this happened to the myth of the Kwai" (Watt 1968, 25).

Boulle's bridge has become a myth that has taken hold of the imagination. Tours are organized from Bangkok to visit "The Bridge over the River Kwai" (presumably reconstructed after the success of the film), and each year thousands of tourists visit this "historic" spot. There is even a hotel adjoining it named "The Inn of the Bridge on the River Kwai." An American mail-order clothing company perpetuates the myth of the bridge in its catalogue, under the rubric "River Kwai," to sell shorts:

> The bridge is there, still. It connects the gorges of Kwai Noi with Kwai Yai. The bridge is sad and strangely excellent and stirring, as you would want it to be. Now, 50 years later, even if you never saw the movie, you can see with your own eyes that this bridge was better constructed than strictly necessary. Thousands of POWs died building it. . . . It is a monument to defiance. It turned the tables. Being built slowly and painstakingly better than it had to be, it became a way of getting back. The bridge became the POW's own agenda, instead of their captors'. Rebellion, especially in any new form, is always worth a trip.[11]

Unlike the myth of the River Kwai, the starting point for *The Test* was a real event, the rescue of a Dutch girl from the Japanese by a Malay family and her subsequent inability to readjust to life in Europe at the end of the war.[12] Like *The Bridge over the River Kwai, The Test* begins during the early months of World War II in the Pacific theater, but the action of the novel is not limited to that period. It continues through the Japanese defeat to the emergence at the end of the war of nationalistic movements seeking to drive the European colonizers from their lands. The war, which is at the heart of *The Bridge over the River Kwai,* here serves merely to trigger the action.

When, after Pearl Harbor, the victorious Japanese invade the Malayan archipelago, massacre the Europeans, and burn their property, Marie Helen, an eight-year-old girl whose mother is in France and whose father has just been killed, escapes the massacre. Pursued into the jungle by the Japanese soldiers, she takes refuge in a kampong, a native village of fishermen, and, terrified, throws her arms around the neck of 15-year-old Moktuy, the eldest son of the most influential man in the kampong. Fearing Japanese reprisals, the father wants to turn Marie Helen over to the Japanese. Moktuy and his mother refuse to do so and arrange to have her stay with them as part of their family. The kindness and tender care of her adoptive family transform the European child into a Malayan girl. She is happy in this life and adopts the customs, beliefs, and superstitions of her new family. She is also irresistibly drawn to Moktuy, who idolizes her. To avoid being uprooted at the end of the war by the Nationalists, who now want to rid Malaya of all Europeans, Marie Helen seeks to convince them that she is indeed Malayan and not European by taking a test they devise. She passes the test, which covers all the customs and laws of the Malays, including their religion, "an amalgam of beliefs borrowed from India, China and Islam, and grafted on to a solid basis of animism, in which Allah shared his kingdom with a multitude of djinns and the mysteriously disembodied spirits haunting the sea and the jungle."[13] To cement the bonds that link her to her Malayan family, she marries Moktuy.

The Europeans return after the end of the war and the young 14-year-old bride is torn from the husband she adores and returned to her mother in France. She is told that after a few years in the world where she is now going to live, when she has passed the necessary test, the baccalauréat, she will be able to act according to her own free will and decide for herself the manner in which she chooses to live. Thus, throughout the four years of preparation for the baccalauréat examination, Marie Helen clings to the hope that she will be permitted to return to Malaya. She believes that passing the white man's test, as she passed the Nationalists' test, will enable her to return to Sinang with Moktuy, who has followed her to France. The young lovers "have hypnotized each other until the baccalauréat has assumed in their eyes the value of a magic parchment, of a golden key which will unlock the door to the realization of their wildest fantasies" (Test, 196–97). They believe that the test assesses one's aptitude for life and love. "This interpretation alone could explain the reason for the high price, which was otherwise inconceivable, that the white men attributed to passing it and the deep disgrace attached to failing" (Test, 198).

Although Marie Helen passed the test of the Malays because that was indeed her culture, she fails the alien "white man's test," centered around mysterious beings named Valéry, Racine, Galileo, Newton, and Ampère. Moktuy, in despair at the thought that they will never be permitted to live together, runs amok,[14] kills her, and finally takes his own life. "The blow she had received had been delivered with the accuracy of madness and the irresistible strength of passion" (*Test,* 214).

Pierre Boulle's years as a planter in Malaya provided the Malayan landscape and atmosphere so vividly realized in this novel of ill-fated love. The remarkable opening chapters convey the atmosphere of a peaceful kampong, a self-sufficient Malayan fishing village on the tropical island of Sinang, only a few miles from Sumatra, where "peace and tranquillity had reigned for several generations. The simple island life required no form of authority or administration. The only directions the fishermen received were from the monsoon and the sea" (*Test,* 9).

Thus it would seem to appear at the outset of the novel that Boulle subscribes to the myth of the noble savage. But for Boulle there are never absolute value judgments. The paradoxes in his work stem from his ability to see both sides of the coin, as is demonstrated by his unflattering portrayal of Ramasamy and the other Malay rubber tappers in *S.O.P.H.I.A.*. Similarly, in *My Own River Kwai,* Boulle expresses surprise that he had once thought that the Thais were a gentle, easy-going people who liked fishing in the river and congregating peacefully in the moonlight and wonders whether his "idyllic first impression of them did not conceal some completely different reality" (*My Own,* 111). That there was also a "completely different reality" hidden behind the imperturbable visage of the Malay fisherman is borne out by Moktuy's fatal violence at the end of the novel. Boulle explains what had set off this violence: "Proud and aloof, like all the fishermen from the islands . . . [Moktuy was] utterly unaffected by the outside world until the day he felt that world had tried to do him harm" (*Test,* 204).

Boulle refutes another odd colonialist notion in *The Test*—one also subscribed to by the American producer of the film *The Bridge on the River Kwai*—which maintains that the ordinary people of Southeast Asia immediately loved the white strangers who came to their lands and would willingly sacrifice themselves on their behalf. On the contrary, the Malay fishermen in *The Test* refuse to help the white men in their desperate flight from the Japanese. Their only concern is for survival, and they are indifferent to the outcome of the war being waged around them. "Protected from the universal madness outside by its supreme indifference and by the lack of any envy to which the modesty of its ambitions could possibly give rise, the kampong . . . continued to lead its same old

monotonous existence, an existence inseparably connected to the age-old
world of the senses and compounded of contemplation and various other
mental outlooks that were completely unaffected by the daily deluge of
natural phenomena. The new Japanese order was as alien to the Malays
as the European organization had been" (*Test*, 58).

Peripheral to the main action in *The Test,* although they act as catalysts
precipitating the tragic dénouement of the novel, are Dr. Moivre and
Father Durelle, members of a post–World War II scientific expedition to
Malaya. Dr. Moivre, who serves here as Boulle's alter ego, expresses the
author's ideas on colonialism. Like his creator, "Moivre would state his
opinion, without ever involving himself personally. It was a long time
since he had felt the urge to subscribe to any particular cause. Whenever
he considered the burning questions of the hour in this part of the world,
he could not avoid the conclusion that, from a strictly moral point of
view, the expropriation of one nation by another could not be justified by
any means or by any argument which had even the remotest claim to
rationalism" (*Test*, 96–97). Dr. Moivre again speaks for Boulle when he
remarks that "the thing that really disgusted him about human degradation was its utterly conventional character which manifested itself in
exactly the same way in every part of the world" (*Test*, 102).

Father Durelle, Moivre's companion on the expedition, is modeled on
Teilhard de Chardin, the French Jesuit, paleontologist, theologian, and
philosopher who tried earnestly to reconcile religious and scientific
dogma. Still, these two honorable men are instrumental in returning
Marie Helen to despair and death in the West. Their action demonstrates once again one of Boulle's basic themes, the absurdity resulting
from the divorce between admirable intentions and deplorable results.
Despite the fact that they note Marie Helen's perfect adaptation to her
milieu, they believe it is their duty to take her back to enjoy the benefits
of the civilization and culture into which she was born and of which she
has been deprived. For surely, Boulle writes with characteristic irony,
"somewhere, scattered abroad, concealed beneath the superficial tinsel
and almost impossible to unearth, there were certain elements of
Western civilization that were more or less worth while" (*Test*, 110). Like
his creator, Moivre remembered having come across two or three himself
in the course of his life, after many years of research.

The Other Side of the Coin follows *The Test* chronologically. It takes place
on a rubber plantation much like Kebun Kessong in *S.O.P.H.I.A.,* but 20
years later. It is "a microcosm of several thousand acres lying across a
region of steep hills, surrounded on all sides by the jungle, inhabited by

black Tamil field hands and yellow Chinese artisans, controlled by three or four sunburned Europeans, and administered by certain far-off paler creatures haunting the City in London or the Bourse in Paris."[15] Changes have occurred, however, in the years since the romantic young planter arrived in Malaya, and the plantation, which "had survived two wars, virulent malaria attacks, whatever damage the beasts of the jungle could inflict on its trees, and the perpetual speculations of Finance as to the future of the white product that flowed drop by drop early every morning from those same trees . . . had been threatened in recent years by a new danger: Chinese terrorism. . . . Directed against the plantation as a whole—it attacked its essence and its principles as an absolute enemy, focusing every effort on the total destruction of the organism" (*Coin,* 11–12).

Initially, it would seem that, whatever changes have occurred, the traditional plantation managerial group of French and English planters has remained the same in this postcolonial period. Their wives are still "condemned to utter idleness in a country where their only social function is to be waited on" (*Coin,* 136), and the romantic young new recruit is still warned against socializing with the natives. But to this traditional cast of characters has been added a new person to reflect the post–World War II American presence in the area, Patricia, the American wife of the manager, Bernard Delavigne.

Patricia, or "Pat," is a stereotypical good-hearted naïve American, secure in the myth of American purity and invincibility, portrayed with a certain affection that harks back to Boulle's bemused admiration for the English in his early novels: "Her moral health was no less apparent than her physical equilibrium. Primarily it was the product of a warm, generous nature instinctively inclined to consider only the noble aspect of human actions. . . . [and] was sustained by the systematic practice of charity and by daily assistance—in both material and spiritual form—accorded the beings around her who were physically and morally less fortunate than she" (*Coin,* 20). Pat declares that "the only effective and honorable way for the advanced nations to deal with the terrorists [menacing the plantation] is to help them out of their poverty and ignorance. All men, including the natives of this country, and the rebels especially, need understanding, love, and sympathy" (*Coin,* 30).

Pat is not meant to be a believable, three-dimensional character any more than Voltaire's Candide. Like all characters in *contes philosophiques,* a genre to which many of Boulle's novels belong, she is the embodiment of the author's ideas, here Boulle's proposition that the best of intentions

can lead to unfortunate consequences and, paradoxically, that unquestioning, complete good can quite innocently create havoc.[16] If the novel
is approached with this understanding, the reader is able to enjoy the
ingenious, rather contrived plot and admire the author's skillful portrayal of human nature, as he juxtaposes Communist terrorists and Western
capitalists, gently mocking the slavish adherence to ridiculous rituals of
both.

During an abortive attack on the plantation by Chinese terrorists, 19-
year-old Ling, the only female and one of the best soldiers in the
Communist camp, is wounded. Patricia finds her in a narrow strip of
jungle separating the bungalow from the plantation, where she has
dragged herself to avoid being taken by the detested whites. Patricia
tells the "houseboy"[17] that they must shelter the girl. "You must forgive
your enemies. You must love them" (*Coin,* 47), she preaches with guile-
less condescension. Three days later, Pat reveals Ling's presence to her
husband, Bernard, explaining that it would be a crime to send the girl
back to "a life of crime and debauchery among a band of lawless fanatics" (*Coin,* 55). If the girl stays with them, she maintains, her bitter feelings will disappear as they teach her "the laws and morality of the
civilized world" (*Coin,* 56). By giving her a Christian education, she adds,
they will know the joy of having saved a soul. Because she believes that
love conquers all, Pat concentrates on that aspect of Christian morality.
"And what did Christ say, Ling?" Pat asks. "Love one another. Love thy
neighbor as thyself for love of Me," Ling replies (*Coin,* 108). Pat's lessons
do bear fruit; love conquers all in a most peculiar fashion. Bernard falls
in love with Pat's Galatea. She, in turn, loves her neighbor's husband for
herself and runs off to Europe with him after arranging to have Pat kid-
napped and held as a hostage by the Popular Army. It would seem that
Pat neglected to include in Ling's "Christian education" Christ's crucial
admonition: "For what shall it profit a man if he shall gain the whole
world and lose his own soul?"[18] Or, perhaps, this was the lesson Ling did
not master.

In *The Other Side of the Coin,* as in most of Boulle's novels, there is a
character who speaks for the author. In *The Bridge over the River Kwai* it
is the medical officer, Major Clipton, and in *The Test,* Dr. Moivre. Here it
is Rawlinson, the district chief of police, who notes initially: "Ling is
beginning to discover our century's more stupefying miracle. . . . that in
our time it is precisely the nations in power who are perfect from every
point of view" (*Coin,* 108–9). He warmly congratulates Pat on her success in having managed to make Ling into a woman of the world. "And

of the best world at that—ours" (*Coin,* 142), he adds in the toneless voice always used by Boulle's spokesmen. He deems her education to be complete—"One of us, that's what she became" (*Coin,* 218)—when she runs off with her benefactor's husband.

Patricia Delavigne is the embodiment of the traditional French view of Americans as overgrown children, no match for the wily Oriental Ling. This persistent French notion is evident in *Ears of the Jungle,* but absent the anti-Americanism usually associated with it, even though the novel deals with the unpopular American war in Vietnam. The novel takes its name from the so-called ears of the jungle, electronic sensors designed to be indistinguishable from jungle vegetation. Boulle explains that he read about these minute monitors dropped by American aircraft over Vietnamese supply routes in the *Armed Forces Journal* of 15 February 1971,[19] and built his novel around them. The sensors pick up the slightest rumble of an engine in their vicinity and transmit it to a central American base in Thailand, where the signals are immediately sorted and analyzed by computers; bombers are then directed to the transmitting area. The sensors and their use by the American forces is authentic, yet, as is his wont, Boulle uses this fact as a point of departure for a cautionary tale in which machines are pitted against human ingenuity.[20]

The North Vietnamese intelligence, headed by Madame Ngha, turn the sensors to their own benefit. Aided by friendly Jarai hill tribesmen and a Chinese electronics genius, Mme Ngha and her comrades triumph over American gadgetry, using the sensors, in a marvelous example of Boulle's extravagant imagination, to direct the destructive agents of technological expertise to serve their own purposes. B-52 bombing raids are trained on the Jarai's hunting grounds, where the game animals killed by the bombs enrich the sparse menus of the tribesmen as well as those of the army. Subsequent napalm attacks clear the underbrush for farming plots and fertilize them with ash for the cultivation of rice and manioc. Finally, the heavy doses of defoliants unleashed over the dense jungle provide a roadbed for the Ho Chi Minh Way, the enlargement of the Ho Chi Minh Trail, which will form the principal postwar link between North and South Vietnam. And, finally, just as the United States Congress cuts off funds for further saturation bombing and chemical defoliation, Mme Ngha uses the sensors to deal the Americans a coup de grâce by directing their last load of bombs back onto their computer center in Thailand.

The tried-and-true formula of turning the tables against the powerful is a staple of folk literature. Mme Ngha is Renart the fox outwitting

Ysengrin the powerful wolf of the medieval fables of *Le roman de Renart,* and all of the characters in the novel are as caricatural as are these anthropomorphic animals. The fabulists expressed no value judgments; they merely delighted in demonstrating how shrewdness, cunning, and intelligence triumphed over brute force. And so it is with Pierre Boulle. He does not present the characters in terms of good and evil—all are *sympathique.* General Bishop, the American commander, is kindhearted and thoughtful and sincerely believes that he is working for future world peace. He is a sensitive human being who responds poetically to the mysterious sounds of the jungle transmitted to him by the sensors. He is also a humane man who paradoxically reprimands the gardener for polluting the environment by spreading weed killer at the base. "That was a period when the civilized world, and especially the United States, was seized by a fever of anxiety and indignation at the idea that mankind, in its disregard for the environment, was everywhere committing unnatural crimes" (*Jungle,* 162), Boulle notes with characteristic irony. Bishop's outburst, moreover, occurs the day after the chemical defoliation of the Vietnamese jungle by American bombers. "While the raids of utter destruction continued over the Ho Chi Minh Trail, General Bishop, won over to the cause from the very beginning, acquainted himself each day with new details of this plague that threatened the world" (*Jungle,* 163). Soon, the idea that biological warfare might after all constitute an act of pollution and an assault on the environment finally crossed the minds of a few important Americans. It finally filtered into the president's office, and "he had only one way to rid himself of it: to declare the end of biological warfare and return to the good old days of saturation bombing with conventional explosives" (*Jungle,* 169).

Boulle's juxtaposition of "good old days" with "of saturation bombing" recalls Voltaire's coupling of "heroic" and "butchery" to describe the battle between the Abares and the Bulgares in *Candide.* The author's casual portrayal of chemical and biological warfare as ordinary, everyday occurrences in the normal order of things recalls the scene in *Candide* in which murder and rape are described as expected behavior by Voltaire's Cunégonde. Unlike other French writers, who attempted to assuage collective French guilt by condemning America's repetition of France's mistakes, Boulle presents war as a universal human blunder. "War acts as a catalyst, or rather as a fertile dung heap that breeds and nourishes to absurd proportions the monstrous flowers of extravagance" (*Jungle,* 223). His target is not the specific war in Vietnam but the absurdity of war in general and of man in particular, that pathetic imbecile so intent on waging it.

Ears of the Jungle is the fifth in a chronological series of novels that take place in the Far East. From the re-creation in *S.O.P.H.I.A.* of the early years of colonialism inherited from the nineteenth century, through World War II (in *The Bridge over the River Kwai* and *The Test*), which was to undermine that colonialism, to the liberation movements unleashed by the war (in *The Test* and *The Other Side of the Coin*), which would put an end to colonialism, and, finally, the casting off of the "white man's burden" (in *Ears of the Jungle*), Boulle provides a historical perspective of Southeast Asia during the first three-quarters of the twentieth century. And yet, despite the dramatic changes that took place during that period, Boulle, without authorial comment and with a philosophical shrug of the shoulders, demonstrates that "plus ça change, plus c'est la même chose," the demon of the perverse remains the driving force behind human behavior.

Chapter Four

Cosmology, Scientific Fiction, Science Fiction

Pierre Boulle's experiences as a planter and a Resistance hero supplied the background and atmosphere for his works situated in Southeast Asia. His scientific education, on the other hand, inspired his essay *L'univers ondoyant* (The undulating universe), a work he defined as a novelist's view of cosmology (Interview, 28 November 1992), as well as a series of science fiction novels and short stories, in particular *Planet of the Apes*—a classic in the science fiction genre and one of the author's finest works. The importance Boulle attaches to the scientific component of his literary production is demonstrated by the epigraph he chose for *L'univers ondoyant,* which is taken from Steven Weinberg's *The First Three Minutes of the Universe:* "The effort to understand the universe is one of the very few things that lifts human life a little above the level of farce, and gives it some of the grace of tragedy."[1]

In the opening paragraphs of the *L'univers ondoyant,* Boulle explains his great interest in cosmology, the study of the birth and history of the universe:

> I have always been fascinated by strange things, and, like the lark dazzled by the perfidious mirror lure of a Provençal hunter, as soon as I think I have seen an unusual scintillation in the jumble of trivial events, I make straight for it, thanking heaven for this rare godsend. . . . Now, a few years ago it seemed to me that the Universe, an entity both material and spiritual, was the strangest subject imaginable, precisely the one to tempt a demanding novelist and to arouse the interest of . . . [the] type of reader . . . who ponders over "the nature of things" and who tries to explore both the body and the soul of the cosmos at the same time.[2]

Scientists almost all agree that the universe began with a Big Bang, an explosive radiation of life forms in which nearly all the major animal groups now on Earth, and others long since extinct, first appeared. But what detonated the explosion? The search for the answer to this question has led Boulle and many would-be metaphysicians to speculate about the larger picture and attempt to construct what might be called cosmic mythology. Boulle bases his theories about the origin and physical nature of the universe on the scientific knowledge of the astrophysicists, emphasizing the fact that it was in fact a novelist, Edgar Allan Poe, who had the first intuition of the Big Bang. In his cosmological essay *Eurêka* of 1848, a so-called transcendental explanation of the universe, Poe took as his point of departure the idea of an initial explosion, and then proposed and developed the theory that the universe must of necessity be in a constant state of dynamic change, alternately expanding and contracting.

Boulle also borrows ideas from different philosophers to fuel his speculations about the spiritual nature of the universe. He was particularly influenced by the Jesuit philosopher and paleontologist Teilhard de Chardin, who tried to reconcile his religious beliefs with his scientific knowledge of evolution, although Boulle himself is "teilhardien without the revelation" (Ganne, 11). Boulle rejects creationism because he is a fervent pantheist and, as such, is firmly convinced that the spiritual and material worlds are indivisible. Nonetheless, he states, "bowing before the amazing discoveries of contemporary science, and also having to admit that the material universe has been in constant flux since an initial explosion, I find myself obliged by these dual convictions to conclude that the Spirit itself is in a state of continual modification and that its nature in this moment is very different from what it must have been before the Big Bang" (*Univers*, 72).

Boulle maintains that the role of the artist is to interpret data as he chooses in order to create a universe to his own measure. Thus, the universe begins to take shape in Boulle's mind as "a perfect material and spiritual unity that was destroyed ten to fifteen billion years ago, with Matter dispersed in corpuscles, and Spirit diffused in these fragments, conserving in each one of them a sort of instinct that one could compare to the instinct of self preservation, and which seeks to find this lost perfection once again" (*Univers*, 76). It would follow then, Boulle continues, that this instinct/memory is ingrained in all the particles of the Universe, and would explain the fact that one finds everywhere—as has already been confirmed by experience—the same atoms, the same molecules, and the same mineral bodies. Boulle does not see how one could otherwise explain this strange fact without postulating the existence of a perfect unity at the outset:[3] "This universality of the laws of nature is considered by certain people to be a solid piece of evidence, if not a proof, that the similarity of structures must not be limited to atoms and molecules, but must continue in many other sectors of the Cosmos including the basic elements of life and of intelligence. I myself some-times have a tendency to go a bit further than the most audacious opti-mist and to dream that thinking beings who inhabit far off planets are not very different materially from human beings at our stage of evolu-tion"(*Univers,* 104).

According to Boulle, then, the universality of the laws of nature would seem to indicate the existence of extraterrestrial civilizations. He believes not only that there are other inhabited planets but also that they are inhabited by minds that exist in bodies like ours. If one accepts the premise of the existence of extraterrestrial civilizations, as well as the assumption that the entire life of the universe is directed toward the goal of returning to the original spiritual and material unity, then contact with these civilizations would be imperative in order to achieve such unity. The necessity to establish contact with extraterrestrial civilizations is at the heart of a great deal of science fiction, which from the very beginning postulated that man undoubtedly was neither the only living being in the universe nor the only one among all the different living species to have reached a high level of development. Boulle's fascination with rockets and spacecraft, like that of many writers of science fiction, can be explained in part by the important role they play in the search for extraterrestrial civilizations. The rocket is, in fact, the vehicle of the modern scientist, "the scientific celestial pole that reaches not to the gods, but to extraterrestrials who will guide humans in their cosmic quest. . . . The scientist is like the shaman, the interpreter of his discov-eries . . . [who] provides a cosmic perspective for modern humanity, [while] . . . the planetary hero is the astronaut who leaves the cradle of our species . . . to explore and transform the space surrounding us and hasten the maturation of mankind."[4]

Le jardin de Kanashima (*Garden on the Moon*) is the story of the birth and development of the rocket, the steed of the astronaut in his cosmic quest. The novel can be classified as scientific fiction rather than science fiction, since it presumes a predominantly pedagogical function. Like the work of Jules Verne, it is directed primarily towards instilling in the reader more or less factual scientific knowledge. Boulle maintains that the real subject here is scientific popularization and that the fiction is the sugar-coated pill. Although three-quarters of the book is little more than a thinly fictionalized compilation of well-known facts, the final 75 pages combine onrushing fact with a slight margin of science fiction, anticipat-ing events that were to take place only five years after its publication.

In the preface to the novel, Boulle comments on the hazards of writing science fiction concurrently with the twists that scientific fact may take. "What I dread is to see the history of tomorrow bring to pass, as it sometimes does, the very absurdities I have tried to avoid."[5] The problems inherent in the extrapolation of contemporaneous scientific knowledge into the immediate future are not limited to potential technical errors; the assassination of President Kennedy, for example, forced Boulle to recast a considerable part of a novel he then believed to be complete. The abrupt removal of Khrushchev, however, happened too late for him to alter his text.

The protagonist of *Garden on the Moon* is another in the cast of monomaniacs who populate Boulle's novels, in this case a rocket scientist named von Schwartz,[6] who is, thinly disguised by a patronymic color change, Wernher von Braun, then the leading rocket scientist in the world; von Braun's V-2 was the first successful ballistic missile. The novel begins in Hitler's Germany at Pennemünde, the German base, where von Schwartz and his staff are making the V-2 rockets designed to wreak devastation over London. They are all young space fanatics: von Schwartz, the doppelgänger of von Braun, and his fictional assistants, including Nadia, daughter of Russian émigrés; Müller, poet turned mathematician; and Kanashima, a Japanese scientist.

If they are making weapons, it is only because there is no other way to finance their experiments; they are more interested in the possibility of sending a rocket to the moon than in perfecting the V-2 rockets to destroy England. Von Schwartz, like his real-life counterpart, sees their role as that of Promethean bearers of a great technological skill for humankind, forged in the fires of war but more important as a means of exploring space than as a weapon. At the beginning of the war, as Boulle reports accurately in his novel, Hitler was not interested in rocket research—German armies were winning with traditional weapons. Still, von Schwartz and his team pushed ahead with the V-2. The first successful launch took place on 3 October 1942, breaking the sound barrier and reaching an altitude of some 55 miles and a range of 120 miles. It was at that moment that the spaceship was born. It was now merely a matter of obtaining more thrust from bigger payloads and achieving greater reliability and accuracy.

In June 1943, with increasingly bad news from the eastern front, Hitler reversed his initial opposition and gave military orders that relieved the Pennemünde scientists of whatever illusions they may have had that they were creating vehicles for space travel. These rockets were to be weapons capable of destroying England. The situation was not without a terrible irony which, strangely, was not exploited by Boulle, the master of irony, caught up perhaps in a shared passion for space exploration.[7] Visionaries they might have been, yet they were working in Nazi Germany and the rockets, which wreaked death and destruction on civilian areas, were manufactured at a nearby site by slave laborers, most of them from Russia. As many as 20,000 laborers are believed to have died building underground factories or making the rockets themselves.[8]

After Germany's defeat, the scientists in the novel are dispersed to different countries: Kanashima to Japan and Nadia to Russia. There she marries a missile expert, a Russian scientist who had been planted as a laborer in the V-2 factory and who is in fact a great rocket expert, the father of the first Sputnik satellite that triggers the superpower race to the moon. In reality, von Braun and his team of German rocket scientists chose America as their future home as the Red Army pushed toward Pennemünde. The Russians picked up the second tier of scientists who had the capacity to reproduce the V-2 but lacked theoretical skills. They made up for this, nevertheless, in the person of their own great rocket scientist, Sergei Korolev.

Von Schwartz goes to the United States but the hopes he pinned on "practical-minded men, men of action, an army of able technicians, a huge industrial potential, and millions of dollars" (*Moon,* 73) are promptly dashed by the little real support given in America. He still continues to plod along with his designs for an interplanetary vehicle, making rockets for the military at the same time. The years pass. Then the Russians launch the Sputnik and the space race is on. Boulle's novel now enters the domain of science fiction, anticipating the landing on the moon that was to be made five years later by the Americans. His description of the rocks and craters of the lunar landscape foretells with amazing accuracy the one given by the astronauts Neil Armstrong and Buzz Aldrin when they landed on the moon on 20 July 1969; it also recalls von Braun's vision of what the moon would be like long before man landed there: "Shadows and images in the strange nightly sunshine will seem haunted by a sense of loneliness."[9] As so often happens, science fiction would soon become reality.

At the same time as the two major powers are vying to be first on the moon, the Japanese scientist Kanashima also has joined the competition. His plan is to win the race to the moon by eliminating all the complicated hardware needed for a return trip to Earth. So that his country may be the first to place a flag on the moon, he takes an astronaut's place for the one way flight, with no possibility of return. During Kanashima's last hours in the strange world evoked by Boulle, far from the chauvinistic egoism and furious competition of the space race, in one of the rare moving moments in science fiction literature, Kanashima, alone in the lunar silence, builds a Zen garden and meditates as he awaits death. "I still have time to dream," he muses. "I say to myself that if I sometimes feel tempted by the arts, basically I do not regret my scientific career. Scientists have now become poets. The proof is that they are beginning to turn their thoughts to the moon" (*Moon,* 311). When his oxygen is exhausted, the scientist has decided to end his life poetically. "In matters of annihilation," he declares, "each has his own ideal. Sailors wish to dissolve in the sea. Certain pantheists ask to be buried without a coffin, stark naked in the soil, in order to mingle as rapidly as possible with the earth. Others wish to be cremated, so that their elements may be dispersed instantaneously in the atmosphere. So, for the conqueror of space, there is no more noble and reasonable ideal than the manner of disintegration on which I have decided" (*Moon,* 312–13). Kanashima plans to make a rent in his space suit, causing his body to explode, hurling clouds of elementary particles in all directions into space at the speed of one mile per second.

> This means that some of my atoms will start orbiting around the moon. Others will even escape its influence. Some of them will be snatched up by planets, and it is not impossible that a few of them will revolve eternally around the earth. Still others, no doubt . . . will become satellites of the sun. And perhaps a few—it is not unreasonable to entertain this hope—a few will escape from the solar attraction through the action of cyclonic disturbances and find their way toward other stars and—who knows?—other galaxies. . . . Whatever happens, it is a fine end for an astronaut. (*Moon,* 313)

Science is the raison d'être of *Garden on the Moon,* but it is ancillary in the remarkably conceived and executed *La planète des singes* (*Planet of the Apes*). While there is also travel in space in this novel, as well as many other themes that are characteristic of science fiction—including travel in time, contact with other civilizations, prehistory, intelligent animals, and the desperately feared end of civilization[10]—it is primarily a work of social criticism reminiscent of Swift and Voltaire. Science fiction and futuristic novels have traditionally been a favorite forum for social critics; they provide an easy means of extrapolating and satirizing the problems of the contemporary world. Rather than disseminating scientific information, the authors of these works are interested in criticizing existing institutions, attacking popular prejudices and morals, and expounding on philosophy and anticipations in science. Boulle considers *Planet of the Apes* to be primarily a work of social criticism and not science fiction, for, he explains, "the apes in that work are as like humans as two peas in a pod; they are in fact human beings. The novel is really a satire; the characters you see in *Planet of the Apes* have nothing in common with the fantastic beings that populate works of science fiction" (Interview, 28 November 1992).

The prologue to *Planet of the Apes* introduces a wealthy couple, Jinn and Phyllis, who are spending a holiday in space at a time when, the author assures us, "interplanetary voyages were an everyday occurrence, and interstellar travel not uncommon."[11] As was often the case in traditional maritime adventure tales, they spy a bottle floating, not in the ocean but in space. When they retrieve the bottle, they discover within it a manuscript, "written in the language of the Earth," which opens with the words: "I am confiding this manuscript to space, not with the intention of saving myself, but to help, perhaps, to avert the appalling scourge that is menacing the human race" (*Planet,* 9).

The journal is the work of Ulysse Mérou, whose name juxtaposes the Homeric hero with a lowly fish, the grouper, undermining from the outset all human pretensions. Mérou, a journalist, embarks in a cosmic ship in the year 2500 with two companions, the misanthropic scientific genius who designed the space craft, Professor Antelle, and his disciple, a young physician named Arthur Levain. Motivated by a desire to escape the human condition, Antelle has chosen a distant galaxy "in the hope of finding a world very different from our own" (*Planet,* 13). He aims to reach the region of space centered around the supergigantic star Betelgeuse.

Traveling at the speed of light minus epsilon for two years, during which three and a half centuries have elapsed on Earth, they land on one of the planets near Betelgeuse, which has the same atmospheric conditions as those on Earth. They name the planet Soror, since it seems to be a sister planet to Earth, resembling it in every way, with oceans, mountains, forests, cultivated fields, towns, and, by extension, inhabitants, whom they have not yet seen. The twin, or sister, planet appears frequently in science fiction, and like its predecessor, the imaginary island, it is a fantastic creation perfectly suited to satirical treatment of humanity (Milling, 92).

On Soror, the space travelers land far from civilization, "in the middle of a plateau, on green grass reminiscent of . . . meadows in Normandy" (*Planet,* 20), and see a naked, beautiful, blond young woman—whom they name Nova—who behaves like an animal and who speaks no language. She is joined by others who also resemble the space travelers physically yet who seem devoid of the power of reason and of speech. What Mérou had found so disturbing when he first saw Nova, and what he finds in the others, is not only a lack of conscious thought but the complete absence of intelligence. "Whenever we had discussed, during the voyage, our eventual encounter with living beings, we saw in our mind's eye monstrous, misshapen creatures of a physical aspect very different from ours, but we always implicitly imagined the presence in them of a *mind*. On the planet Soror reality appeared to be quite the reverse: we had to do with inhabitants resembling us in every way from the physical point of view but who appeared to be completely devoid of the power of reason" (*Planet,* 38–39).

As Mérou and his companions observe these humans, they are attacked by hunters, who are apes dressed like men, hunting like men, and acting like men. In these animals' eyes, Mérou sees the spark of understanding he had sought in vain among the human inhabitants of Soror. In the course of the hunt, Levain is killed, Antelle disappears, to reappear later in a cage in a zoo, and Mérou is caught in a trap, taken prisoner with other human prisoners, placed in a cage, and loaded onto a cart. The fate of the three men parallels that of animals on Earth; they are either hunted and killed for sport like Levain, incarcerated in zoos like Antelle, or subjected to experiments in scientific laboratories like Mérou. These stupefying events lead Mérou to exclaim, "I was a man, I mean a man from Earth, a reasoning creature who made it a habit to discover a logical explanation for the apparently miraculous whims of nature, and not a beast hunted down by highly developed apes" (*Planet,* 69–70). Like Voltaire's tale *Micromégas,* Boulle's novel mocks humankind's anthropocentric theory of the universe from which human beings derive their sense of importance.

Mérou and the other humans in their cages are subjected to various cruel and unnecessary tests, not unlike those used in animal experimentation on Earth. First, their reflexes are studied, then their level of intelligence, and, finally, their sexuality. Men and women are paired in cages to permit the study in captivity of their amorous practices, the methods of approach of the male and the female, and the manner in which they copulate. Mérou is paired with Nova. The men indulge in a display similar in every way to that executed by certain birds: dancing, circling, and approaching. When the apes notice that Mérou, who had sworn that nothing would induce him to make such a spectacle of himself, is not participating, they prod him with their pikes. "I, Ulysse Mérou," he exclaims, "a man created in the image of God! I resisted them energetically" (*Planet,* 102). But, overcome with jealousy when Nova is placed in a cage with another man, he relents. He explains: "I, one of the kings of creation, started circling around my beauty—I, the ultimate achievement of millennial evolution, in front of this collection of apes eagerly watching me . . . I, a man, excusing myself on the grounds of exceptional cosmic circumstances, and persuading myself for the moment that there are more things on the planets and in the heavens that have ever been dreamed of in human philosophy, I, Ulysse Mérou, embarked like a peacock around the gorgeous Nova on the love display" (*Planet,* 105).

Mérou becomes more and more comfortable with his life in captivity. During the day the apes tend to his every need, and at night he shares his "litter with one of the loveliest females in the cosmos" (*Planet,* 109). One day, however, he feels ashamed of his cowardly resignation, determines to behave like a civilized man, and begins to learn the simian language and customs with the help of a female scientist named Zira. Again, satirizing human pretension by placing our clichés into the mouths of apes, Boulle has Mérou ask Zira whether apes are the only rational beings, the sovereigns of creation on her planet. She replies: "Ape is of course the only rational creature, the only one possessing a mind as well as a body. The most materialistic of our scientists recognize the supernatural essence of the simian mind" (*Planet,* 116).

Zira tells Mérou that there are three different classes among the apes, gorillas, orangutans, and chimpanzees, each of which has its own characteristics. The division of authority among the apes on Soror mirrors human social divisions. The gorillas have a taste for authority and form the most powerful class. They are cunning and know how to exploit the inventions of other apes. Those among them who do not occupy positions of authority are engaged in occupations requiring physical strength. They are also the hunters who capture humans for experimentation. The orangutans represent official science; they are the enemies of progress. "Pompous, solemn, pedantic, devoid of originality and critical sense, intent on preserving tradition, blind and deaf to all innovation, they form the substratum of every academy. Endowed with a good memory, they learn an enormous amount by heart and from books. Then they themselves write other books, in which they repeat what they have read, thereby earning the respect of their fellow orangutans" (*Planet,* 140). The chimpanzees represent the intellectual element of the planet, and it is Zira and her fellow chimpanzee scientists who befriend Mérou.

Mérou becomes accepted by the scientific community on Soror, and one of the young scientists invites him to join an archaeological expedition to a remote region on the planet. At the dig they find traces of a human civilization essentially similar to the present ape civilization on Soror. This would seem to indicate that human beings once reigned as masters on the planet and that a civilization, like the one Mérou left on Earth, had flourished on Soror more than 10,000 years before. It would also suggest that the humans had degenerated and reverted to an animal state, while the apes, through diligence and assertiveness, had copied the humans as they were originally and become their masters. Conclusive proof of this hypothesis is provided by the great scientist, Professor Antelle, who, Mérou discovers, has reverted in captivity to an animal state. Professor Antelle embodies the failure of human scientific achievements and demonstrates that through disuse intelligence can atrophy. On Soror, the human race had been destroyed by apathy rather than by war or pestilence. It had stagnated and permitted the apes to take its place in a nonanthropocentric universe. Mérou concludes that the importance the apes attach to biological research probably originated in the past, when they served as experimental subjects for humans.

The fear of human extinction has often been expressed in science fiction in terms of domination by creatures from other planets, by robots, or even by computers, but in *Planet of the Apes,* humankind is replaced by an inferior species, lower on the evolutionary ladder. Like the Houyhnhnms in Swift's *Gulliver's Travels,* the race of horses who are creatures of pure reason, animals have taken the place of humans, whom they regard as inferior creatures. In *Planet of the Apes,* homo sapiens, homo faber, has become extinct. This pessimistic view of the future is shared by many contemporary science fiction authors and is very different from the optimistic themes of earlier science fiction writers like Arthur C. Clarke, who are faithful to a boyhood vision of science as savior of humankind, and of humankind as a race of potential gods destined for the stars.

Boulle's novel, in which some of the most telling attacks are directed against established science as represented by the orangutans, reflects rather a certain malaise, discomfiture, and fear of science. It is closer to the pessimistic outlook of H. G. Wells, who demonstrated his belief that modern society carries within it the seeds of an inevitable decline, if not a catastrophe. This basic pessimism was extended by Wells in *The Island of Doctor Moreau* to the evolution of science and, finally, to evolution itself. "I look about me at my fellow men; and I go in fear," he wrote. "I see faces keen and bright; others, dull or dangerous: others unsteady, insincere,—none that have the calm authority of a reasonable soul. I feel as though the animal was surging up through them; that presently the degradation of the Islanders will be played over again on a larger scale."[12]

When Mérou returns after the expedition to the scientific institute where he now conducts research, it seems to him that the humans recognize him, and he decides that destiny has brought him to Soror to be the instrument of human regeneration. His heroic mission is aborted, unfortunately, when Nova gives birth to a baby boy who cries like a human infant rather than an animal, and he and his family are forced to leave Soror because the ape population regards them as a danger to the simian race. "It's not possible!" Mérou cries. "I who believed myself entrusted with a semi-divine mission! I feel I am once again the most wretched creature living and give way to the most dreadful despair" (*Planet*, 236–37).

With the aid of Zira and another chimpanzee, they escape in a spaceship and, after a few years that are centuries on Earth, they return there, eagerly anticipating a reunion with intelligent human beings. Instead, they are greeted by gorillas in the same state of development as the apes they had left on Soror. The evolutionary degeneration of humans on Soror has been duplicated on Earth. Indeed, it has been duplicated everywhere in the cosmos. The simian nature of the couple in the prologue—who discover Mérou's journal and express their astonishment at his use of words like "the human race" (*Planet*, 9) and "human beings" (*Planet*, 10)—is revealed in the epilogue,[13] where they conclude that the journal is the work of a poet or a practical joker: "Rational men? Wise men? Men inspired by intelligence? . . . No, that's not possible; there, the story teller went too far. But it's a pity."[14]

Planet of the Apes is not only a fascinating story, it is a also a satirical work in which the apes are not monsters; they are merely men and women in disguise with all of the strengths and weaknesses of human nature. Boulle's view presented here is that another species replaced us on the evolutionary ladder. The human race did not destroy itself; rather, it apathetically permitted the simians to take its place below the angels in the great chain of being.

All philosophical inquiry and all social criticism have been ignored by the makers of the film *Planet of the Apes*,[15] who, unfortunately, converted the novel into what is called "space opera," a type of fiction midway between bad science fiction and nonscience fiction, patterned on the western and containing diverse elements taken from the fairy or fantastic tale. While science in the novel facilitates the discussion of social and philosophical questions by transporting the protagonist to another planet, in the film it becomes merely science fiction paraphernalia—a spaceship that crashes at the beginning of the film and is never seen or heard of again.

The film opens on board an American spaceship as Captain Taylor is dictating his notes: "Six months in deep space, out of Cape Kennedy. Year earth time 2673, ship time 1972. I leave the twentieth century with few regrets. Space is boundless, it squashes a man's ego. Does man, that glorious paradox who sent me to the stars still make war on his neighbor?" The dialogue throughout the film continues in an unbroken string of similar verbal clichés, paralleled by many cinematographic clichés, among them the death of the beautiful blond female astronaut who, because of a hole in her air supply, next appears as a desiccated corpse straight out of the 50-year-old movie *Lost Horizon*.

There is no landing on a "sister planet" as in the novel, but there is a terrible crash with cataclysmic cinematic effects. Water comes rushing into the cabin, and the men abandon "ship" and take off on a rubber raft. Then they are shown walking along in the desert, outlined against the vast sky of the typical cowboy film. Like most westerns, the film contains many chase sequences, including the hunting scene from the novel, but here, in a change approved by Boulle, the apes are on horseback instead of on foot as in the traditional hunting beat he described in the novel.[16] While in the novel Mérou had to learn the highly refined language of his captors, the hero's inability to communicate with the anglophone apes in the film is blamed on a throat wound he received during the hunt. His colleague's reversion to an animal state, which echoed the degeneration of the human race in the novel, is explained here as the result of a lobotomy performed on him by the apes.

The dénouement of the film is equally unsatisfactory. Aided by friendly chimpanzees ("good" Indians) and chased by hostile gorillas and orangutans ("bad" Indians), Taylor and Nova escape on horseback across the American western landscape. After a series of shootouts, with apes falling from horses and off cliffs, they find themselves on a beach. Before them, buried in the sand, is part of the Statue of Liberty.[17] "Oh my God, I'm back, I'm home," the hero exclaims. "All the time it was. . . . We finally really did it, you maniacs, you blew it up, damn you all to hell!"

This conclusion was dictated by the producers of the film, who felt the need for something more dramatic—or perhaps psychologically more acceptable—than apathy to explain the collapse of human civilization, and decided on a nuclear war, a convention of the time.[18] While Pierre Boulle disapproved of the film, [19] because it ignored the philosophical and social questions at the heart of his work, he was particularly critical of the ending, which even did away with the notion of space travel by indicating that the protagonist had, in fact, never left Earth.

The novel *Planet of the Apes* is disquieting because it reflects the eternal human fear of the end of the world, or at least of the world we know. Here, as is often the case in science fiction, science has replaced religion in the search for the origin and destiny of the human species; it is, in fact, an existential search for answers to the questions of creation and existence. Unlike the religious quest, however, the quest in science fiction is affected by the fear of what we may discover, the fear that the gods we have created to save us may fail us and that, far from bringing the anticipated solution to all human ills, science might, like Frankenstein's monster, turn against and destroy its creators. Pessimism about the future of humanity, uncertainty about the purpose and meaning of existence, and fear of the destructive power of science all contribute to the malaise, even anguish, produced by Boulle's novel. This disquiet pervades much contemporary science fiction and often finds expression in the dystopia, one of the darker varieties of science fiction.

Les jeux de l'esprit (*Desperate Games*) is a work of antiutopian science fiction that springs from our disappointment in the promises of a scientific utopia and, particularly, from the fear that progress will carry us into some nightmare world in which the power of technology directed by cold intellect will be supreme. The dystopia depicted in *Desperate Games* reflects our conscious and unconscious apprehension of threats to our integrity and well being, threats made all the more terrifying by the technology that increasingly dominates our lives.

The novel postulates a world in the first part of the twenty-first century taken over by scientists who decide that society is being ruined, mostly because of the stupid vanities of politicians, and feel that it is their duty as rational human beings to intervene. "The scientists had come to regard themselves as the one true international body, the only valid one, based on knowledge and understanding. Science, they felt, was both the soul of the universe and the single force capable of fulfilling human destiny once having wrested mankind from the trivial, infantile preoccupations of ignorant, verbose politicians. [There] gradually . . . emerged the vision of a glorious future, a planet united at last under the guidance of learning and wisdom."[20]

During the first three years of the scientific world government, nationalism vanishes, the concept of the world citizen is dominant, and war has become an impossibility. The world's population has been stabilized, "permitting rational exploitation of resources without waste and without want" (*Games* , 85). Everyone is suitably housed, famine and hunger disappear as well as disease and most of the other ills of humanity. During the next three years, the scientists turn away from the physical problems to take a look at the spiritual side of human life and set about giving everyone a scientific education. "For them, Science was a philosophy, verging on a religion: a religion whose enigmatic and presently inaccessible God was the essence of the Universe; whose sole acknowledged rite was unceasing research; whose creed [was] the knowledge of this universe" (*Games,* 43–44).

Unfortunately, people cling to their ignorance. When the world's greatest astronomer gives a lecture on the stars, the auditors want to know how the knowledge will affect their horoscopes; an explanation by a renowned physicist of the basic structure of the atom—that all bodies eventually reduce to the same physical properties—generates questions on how to transmute common elements into gold. Similarly, lectures on statistics and probability engender questions on an infallible system for winning at roulette. And, even worse, the masses get bored, triggering an outbreak of suicides. Overreliance on machines that think and act for them induces in people a malady diagnosed as LCE, "loss of confidence in the ego"[21] (*Games,* 127). This loss of self-confidence is the result of their having transferred that confidence to the devices provided by science.

Desperately trying to maintain a remnant of interest in science among their subjects, the leaders feel obliged to provide the distractions that will ward off the boredom of utopian living. Here we find another variation on Boulle's theme of the absurd consequences of the best of intentions. A series of diversions that are more and more violent, the so-called "games," are instituted; these are a series of savagely inhuman public spectacles in which competitors fight to the death. The leaders are constrained to reinvent what they had abolished: wars, massacres, genocides. By this time, scientists have been drawn into the popular fervor, science has become debased, and the old physics/biology schism becomes deadly in these games as bacteriological warfare retaliates for nuclear bombing. Boulle's prophetic vision of dystopia is reminiscent of that set

forth in 1948 by Aldous Huxley in *Ape and Essence:* "From the very beginning of the industrial revolution He [the Devil] foresaw that men would
be made so overweeningly bumptious by the miracles of their own technology that they would soon lose all sense of reality. And that's precisely
what happened. These wretched slaves of wheels and ledgers began to
congratulate themselves on being the Conquerors of Nature. Conquerors
of Nature, indeed! In actual fact, of course, they had merely upset the
equilibrium of Nature and were about to suffer the consequences."[22]

Isaac Asimov, one of the masters of science fiction, would take some
improbable scientific premise as his point of departure and then weave a
self-consistent, scientifically reasonable story around it. Boulle, on the
other hand, starts from a more or less probable scientific premise and
then puts in motion a rigorously logical chain of reactions to produce an
improbable result. In four formulaic science fiction novels, the author
demonstrates that however admirable the scientific goal may be—desperately needed sources of energy in *L'énergie du désespoir* (The energy of
despair), *Miroitements* (*Mirrors of the Sun*), and *Le bon Léviathan* (*The Good
Leviathan*), or a cure for breast cancer in *Le professeur Mortimer* (Professor
Mortimer)—the methods used to achieve the goal gradually pervert the
original intention and lead to an ill-fated dénouement.

"I am an illustrator of ideas," Boulle states. "I look for easily verifiable
scientific ideas or theories, and then I present them as simply as possible."[23] The idea behind *L'énergie du désespoir,* according to Boulle, is a scientific theory propounded by Dr. Brian D. Josephson, co-winner of the
1973 Nobel Prize in physics and an outspoken believer in spiritualism,
who thinks that science is on the verge of discovering a new type of energy. This energy will be produced by poltergeists, or spirits, which are
assumed to be the explanation for rapping and other unexplained dis-
placements of matter.[24] Boulle based his novel *L'énergie du désespoir* on this
scientifically tenuous premise.

The novel, like many science fiction novels, is cast in the mold of the
Gothic or post-Gothic novel of the late eighteenth and early nineteenth
centuries, a style of fiction characterized by a murky atmosphere of horror, gloom, irrational violence, desolation, and decay, as well as by
grotesque, macabre, and fantastic incidents.[25] The narrator is a journalist
who has come to a desolate region of France to convalesce from a recent
illness and to complete a novel. "Thrust by chance into this universe of
the absurd," he is merely "an ingenuous witness: an unimportant character. He resembles me like a brother,"[26] Boulle explains.

In the midst of the deserted landscape in which he finds himself stands a large, isolated compound, a sanatorium cum prison that the peasants claim to be haunted because of the strange noises heard there every night. It seems to be bathed in an atmosphere of melancholy and anguish and resembles a sinister fortress, consisting principally of two enormous identical gray concrete buildings, which house separately, behind bars and wire fencing, 1,000 boys and girls between the ages of 13 and 18. Even more ominous is the enormous electric power line leading into the compound, one that would be capable of supplying energy to a small city.

The narrator quotes from Poe's *Fall of the House of Usher* to describe his feelings on first sight of the buildings: "A sense of insufferable gloom pervaded my spirit. . . . There was an iciness, a sinking, a sickening of the heart—an unredeemed dreariness of thought. . . . There are combinations of very simple natural objects which have the power of thus affecting us" (*Energie*, 25). At that moment, he continues, "I had a vague intuition that everything here, from the choice of the site, the planning and construction of the buildings, everything to the slightest detail had been carefully calculated and planned to create an unhealthy atmosphere of anguish and turmoil" (*Energie*, 28).

In harmony with this forbidding establishment is its director, the mysterious professor Trouvère,[27] like so many of Boulle's protagonists "a strange mixture of poet and polytechnician, both a scientist of genius and an insane monster" (*Energie*, 28). Trouvère's assistant, Martha, an ill-favored, mannish German psychiatrist, also appears to have stepped out of a Gothic novel.

The journalist's suspicion that the atmosphere is calculated to foster and intensify the inner torment of the boys and girls is confirmed when Professor Trouvère explains to him the nature of his establishment. To produce energy through poltergeists, he deems it necessary to provoke and then frustrate desires in certain somewhat abnormal pubescent boys and girls. When these young people are thus stimulated, they can give a considerable physical stimulus to matter. Trouvère's premise is that if one person has the gift of producing these phenomena, then 10 people of the same sort can create energy 10 times stronger, and so forth. "I will succeed in producing incomparably greater energy if my plans for the future are realized, which I do not doubt; a mental energy that has its source in the brain, a clean, pure energy which does not poison the atmosphere like coal or oil, which entails no risk like nuclear energy, energy which bursts forth entirely from an immaterial, odorless, invisible bundle of repressed desires" (*Energie,* 72–73).

Trouvère leads the journalist through his establishment, which contains the archetypal mad scientist's laboratory, in this case with enormous wattmeters, a "pavilion of electrical thought," and other devices for the conversion of psychic into electrical energy. "No technical progress can justify this intrusion into a diabolical universe. . . . No human being can stir up these evil powers with impunity" (*Energie,* 134), the narrator tells the mad genius, adding that such concourse will lead inevitably to an uncontrollable catastrophe. And, indeed, his prediction comes to pass. Alix and Marc, two of Trouvère's most promising subjects, produce a horrendous surge of power by combining their almost miraculous poltergeist powers. Professor Trouvère is electrocuted; the two buildings, torn from their foundations, slide towards each other and fuse, uniting the boys and girls; and Alix and Marc break away from the buildings and fly away.

L'énergie du désespoir is similar to one of Edgar Allan Poe's terrifying tales of horror. There is no mystery or suspense, however, in *Mirrors of the Sun.* Like the novels of Jules Verne, it seeks to disseminate factual scientific knowledge, in this case details about the production of solar energy. The putative source of energy in *L'énergie du désespoir* is poltergeists. In *Miroitements,* however, it is the sun. Despite these differences, both novels repeat the leitmotif of Boulle's work; the best intentions sometimes result in perfect contradiction to the pure sentiments that inspired the act.

Jean Blondeau, an environmentalist, has been elected president of France. His campaign speech attacking pollution and the concomitant environmental degradation reads like a tract and is particularly ironic in terms of the outcome of his actions. To achieve his goal of eradicating pollution, he devotes all of the efforts of his administration to the construction of Helios, a gigantic solar installation destined to bring to France's entire population an inexhaustible source of nonpolluting energy. Supported by his ministers and especially his wife—a passionate devotee of the sun—Blondeau embarks on this magnificent venture with an almost religious fervor; his is a crusade to sanctify solar energy.

There is no questionable pseudoscience here as there is in *L'énergie du désespoir.* The tower-system process of generating electricity by solar power is described with scientific accuracy. It consists of "an array of ordinary flat, or else slightly curved mirrors called heliostats. . . . Sunlight striking these heliostats is reflected and focused on the cavity of a boiler mounted atop a tower some three hundred feet high. Computerized clockwork keeps the mirrors rotating very slowly around both a horizontal and a vertical axis as they follow the sun's path, so that at any given moment between sunrise and sunset the reflected rays focus on the boiler. This causes a significant rise in the heat-transfer fluid" (*Mirrors*, 42–43). Solar radiation thus drives the turbine, which runs the alternator that delivers electric power to the system. Perfection, indeed!

Those familiar with Boulle's work can anticipate the failure of such a great enterprise; the projected utopia degenerates ultimately into a dystopia. The first hint of trouble comes with the discovery by the fisherman Pauleau of increasing numbers of sick and dying fish with pink spots on their bellies. Their death is caused by contaminated water from the central canal adjoining the plant, whose waters are being discharged into all its subsidiary waterways. The water is polluted with toxic detergents used to remove the grime that collects on the heliostats each day. Since the plant's energy output is tied to an optical system dependent on the reflective power of the heliostats, which can function efficiently only if free of foreign matter, the heliostats must remain clean.

The heliostats are also befouled with the droppings of flocks of birds captivated by the dazzling sunlight they reflect. Drawn to them as they are to the perfidious mirror lures of Provençal hunters, the birds not only prevent the sunlight from falling on the heliostats, but they also often approach the mirrors too closely and are burned to a crisp. President Blondeau reluctantly grants permission to poachers to kill the birds; the bird population is gradually wiped out, and the solar plant temporarily improves its output. Unfortunately, the disappearance of the birds brings with it another plague, the proliferation of insects that the birds would normally eat. Dense clouds of insects now cover the heliostats and severely diminish their effectiveness, as did the birds before them. Once again, in desperation, the ecologist president betrays his ideals and agrees to extensive spraying with DDT. Torn between the terror of having to admit a searing defeat and the guilt he bears for the devastation of the environment, Blondeau becomes increasingly disturbed; he is no longer fit to govern. Ironically, it is his well-intentioned efforts that have produced the dire results he warned against in his campaign address.

Deserted by his ministers, who are mounting a campaign against him, he sets off with his wife in his solar plane—science fiction that is yet to become reality—and circles above the plant in an ecstatic fantasy. Like Icarus, in a dénouement quite at variance with the realism of the novel, he flies too close to the sun:

The solar craft looked like a giant bird gliding on outstretched wings, captivated by the dazzling reflections of a mirror. . . . Rising nearly three hundred feet above the heliostats, as some of the birds had done, the plane drew very close to one of the boilers, traversing the zone in which the convergent rays from forty thousand mirrors created a furnace heated to some thousand degrees. . . . [The] craft disintegrated all at once, its fragile body, its immense wings dotted with voltaic cells bursting into flames like a torch. All that remained of what floated down through the air for an instant was a smoldering pile of liquified metal, some shapeless bits of debris that came to rest on the shimmering sea of heliostats, desecrating for one last time the blazing splendor of this shrine of the sun. (*Mirrors,* 182–83)

While the third exemplary science fiction novel, *Le professeur Mortimer,* like *Mirrors of the Sun,* is built on a scientifically sound base—a cure for breast cancer that combines varying amounts of interleukin-2 with chemotherapy, radiation, transplants, and grafts—the setting, atmosphere, and protagonist also bear the mark of the Gothic novel and are particularly reminiscent of *The Island of Doctor Moreau* of H. G. Wells. Boulle, like Wells more than 50 years before him, debates in this work the moral, social, and scientific implications of new discoveries in the field of biology. Although science has contributed to widespread compassion for animals by revealing humanity's physical and emotional kinship with them, it has also resorted to vivisection as a tool of scientific discovery, thus undermining faith in science as an instrument of moral progress and causing deep divisions between the proponents of scientific progress and the defenders of animal rights.

Like Wells's Dr. Moreau, the eponymous Professor Mortimer is a renowned surgeon and, at the same time, a mad scientist, a strange mixture of good and evil, torn between the benign persona of Dr. Jekyll and his mad alter ego Mr. Hyde. He is yet another of Boulle's ambiguous heroes, tormented by the "demon of perversity" (*Frédéric,* 13) that drives him to act in direct contradiction to his basic nature, often performing dangerous, painful, at times fatal experiments on animals in the course of his research. At the height of his career, Mortimer suddenly decides to give up clinical medicine to devote himself completely to perfecting a cure for breast cancer. He retires with a few of his assistants, his wife, and his beloved dog, Rosetta, to a deserted island where he can experiment on animals until his cure is proved safe for human beings. In science fiction plots, remote islands, like distant planets, present either an alternative to or an analogue of the "real world" from which the hero embarks. Opposed to the civilized world, the island represents the idyllic primeval garden or, as in *Le professeur Mortimer,* a hellish inversion of paradise where the hero's humanity is destroyed by uncontrollable forces.

Mortimer's mysterious behavior alerts Miss Bridget, an old spinster who has devoted her life to the protection of animals. She is certain that illegal animal vivisection is taking place on the island. The opposition between this fierce friend of animals and the vivisectionist Mortimer is ironic, for these enemies are mirror images of one another in their insane preference for animals over humans.

Strange things are indeed happening on the island, but not what Bridget believes. When Mortimer's beloved dog Rosetta develops breast cancer, he finds that he can no longer experiment on dogs or other animals, since they resemble Rosetta too closely, and works on humans instead. Ultimately, he is able to cure his human patient, yet fails to save his dog. When she dies, he goes mad with grief and plunges a stylet through the heart of the woman he has cured. The final scene describes the Götterdämmurung of Mortimer's island as the mad professor releases all of the animals and sets fire to his clinic. As the flames illuminate the outline of his tall body stumbling over the rocks, giving the impression of a "disjointed puppet struggling across the white-hot twigs that the fire spread around him, or of a gigantic sprite leaping about among the fireflies of an accursed world,"[28] he throws himself off a cliff and takes with him the secret of the cure.

A young psychologist serves as chorus in the novel, commenting on the events and explaining Mortimer's abnormal behavior as the result of a conflict between the conscious and the subconscious, another of the basic themes in Boulle's work. The conscious side prided itself on the admirable research the doctor was performing for the good of humanity. That was the excuse it gave to the irrational side of his strange personality. It was his subconscious, however, tormented from the beginning of his career by the terrible feelings he had when he experimented on animals, that dictated the majority of his actions. Little by little the subconscious became the master, destroying Dr. Mortimer's work, little by little Doctor Jekyll disappeared, absorbed completely by Mr. Hyde.

The Good Leviathan pits environmentalists against oil and nuclear polluters as inconclusively as *Le professeur Mortimer* opposes fanatic animal right's activists to medical researchers. Boulle's aim here, as in many of his works, is to disquiet his readers by making them aware both of the existence of certain problems as well as of the absence of satisfactory solutions. He seeks to sow confusion in the reader's mind by clouding the issue and by undermining principles formerly believed to be immutable. By encouraging the reader to see all sides of an issue, Boulle teaches a lesson of tolerance. Yet he also reminds us that all things are not absolutely equal, and he makes a distinction between thinking ecologists, horrified by the "ever expanding abominations of a world disfigured by the machine and poisoned by chemistry," and those who, at any opportunity, however flimsy, "rise up in fury against the slightest change made to nature caused by the hand of man," loudly proclaiming at the same time "the right to exist of mosquitoes, rats, wolves, mad dogs, and poisonous mushrooms, for the simple reason that these are natural elements of our environment."[29]

Like its predecessors *Mirrors of the Sun* and *L'énergie du désespoir*, *The Good Leviathan* centers around the desperate need for new sources of energy. The protagonist of the novel is Gargantua, the largest nuclear-powered supertanker ever built, capable of carrying 600,000 tons of oil. Universally feared because of concern about radioactive emissions as well as gigantic oil spills, the supertanker is nicknamed the Leviathan, "the name of a creature spewed out of hell" (*Leviathan*, 3). Equipped with a unique foghorn, which it has to sound continually like a leper's warning bell, Gargantua is harassed by a horde of environmental activists who follow this pestilential ship wherever it goes. Chief among its enemies is a lame woman, a former factory worker crippled in an accident she ascribes to the lack of a system of safeguards. Her suffering has fostered in her a fierce hatred for every advance in science, particularly the Leviathan, which she claims to be an instrument of the devil.

When the Gargantua returns from the Near East loaded with oil, a fleet of small boats surrounds it. At a signal, those on the lame woman's boat rush forward to board the tanker, prompting the captain to have his men turn hoses of water on them. The attackers are terrorized by the supposedly poisoned water, which in truth has never passed through the reactor and is sea water drawn up by circulation pumps to cool the condensers. The lame woman receives a full blast of water and, as a result of the shock, her knotted body unbends and her deformed hip straightens, as her eyes reflect the adoration of one touched by a miracle who sees signs invisible to other mortals. The startled observers uncover their heads and kneel. And thus "the monstrous nuclear tanker, symbol of material progress, fruit of the labor of an army of scientists, engineers, and technicians working on the theories of a physicist of genius formulated three quarters of a century earlier" (*Leviathan*, 100), becomes in a few days a destination for pilgrims seeking cures from its water, a liquid now more sacred than any from holy water fonts. A spa with a town around it is built adjoining the tanker, and the Gargantua proceeds to divide its time equally between its miraculous functions and its original purpose of carrying oil, satisfying thereby two imperious needs of humanity—the need for fuel and the need for faith.

The ecologists now disregard the peril posed by nuclear propulsion and concentrate their wrath on the "poison" the ship is carrying, the oil that could at any moment spread out in a deadly tide over thousands of square miles of ocean. They follow the Gargantua everywhere in their small boat, hoping to catch it in some violation, but maintenance is perfect and leaks virtually nonexistent. When the Gargantua and its shadow are off the coast of Africa, a great storm comes up and, at the request of the ecologists, whose boat is in serious difficulty, the Gargantua spreads oil to calm the troubled waters, saving the lives of the ecologists as well as of passengers on all craft in the area. Good and evil have changed places as the Leviathan plunges into the African night "to distribute the benefits of its redemptive black tide on a dream sea" (*Leviathan,* 204). In this novel, written after the terrible accident in which the *Amoco-Cadiz* spilled 250,000 tons of oil on the coast of Brittany causing an environmental disaster, Boulle displays the skill and the wit to write a novel about an environmental polluter and offer a sympathetic view of the polluter. Taking a lesson from Tolstoy, who once said that he had the most success with his stories when the reader didn't know which side he was on, Boulle once again refuses to conclude. He conveys to the reader, nevertheless, his tacit condemnation of all excess and his insistence on the relativity of good and evil, a theme he has tried to exemplify in most of his novels and short stories (Interview, 28 November 1992).

Boulle's works of science fiction range in quality from the extraordinary *Planet of the Apes* to the repetitive formulaic novels that read like textbook demonstrations, distinguishable only by the problem treated. They are marked by a diversity of subject matter—from a novelist's vision of cosmology, to the creation of a scientific dystopia, to space travel to the moon and to a planet inhabited by thinking apes, to havoc wrought by alternate sources of energy. Despite these differences, all are in keeping with the definition that categorizes science fiction as "the literary genre that explores and dramatizes the implications of scientific theory and knowledge, and that treats the cosmological questions raised by scientific investigation within the context of traditional mythic models and literary patterns" (Milling, 43).

Chapter Five
Short Stories and Philosophical Tales

Pierre Boulle divides his oeuvre into two parts—the first part consisting of novels, the second of short stories and philosophical tales. While all of his works share certain interests, and both the novels and the short works of fiction demonstrate a preference for particular themes, there are some differences between the genres. Boulle has commented on these differences. When he writes a novel, he remarks, he attempts to make the plot as plausible as possible, but this is not the case in the short works. There he concentrates on inventing a surprise ending, which he writes first, and then he organizes all plot elements to lead to that ending (Interview, 28 November 1992). While Boulle eschews detailed expositions and psychological analyses throughout his oeuvre, and all of his plots are accessible and technically straightforward in the telling, his technique is particularly suited to the short story, where plot is the only imperative and where there is no place for long developments. In fact, many of the novels would have benefited from being pared down to the dimensions of the short story. The stories are ambitious in the variety of experiences with which they deal and the subjects they explore.

Pierre Boulle's first collection of short stories is titled *Contes de l'absurde* (Tales of the absurd),[1] but his definition of the absurd excludes all connotations of existential philosophy. There is no divorce here between a meaningless universe governed purely by chance and a human desire for order and meaning. Rather than absurd, the stories are paradoxical, fantastic, strange; they lead to absurd conclusions that result when logic is carried to the extreme. Four of the five stories in the collection are built on certain basic themes in science fiction: time travel; the wonders of science and its opposite, uncontrolled technology; the relationship between man and machine; and cataclysm resulting from changing physical conditions. The stories are not of equal quality—some tend toward preciosity, others telegraph their "surprise" endings, and the false naïveté of others seems designed specifically to invite the reader's complicity and admiration—but they are for the most part technically competent and

well written. Among the best, and considered to be one of the classics of
the genre,[2] is "Une nuit interminable" ("Time out of Mind"),[3] which
develops all the variations, implications, and paradoxes of the science fiction theme of a voyage in time. This story demonstrates the way in
which Boulle's irony separates him from most science fiction writers; he
realizes that humor is necessary to make the extraordinary acceptable
and to keep the unbelievable from becoming ridiculous. He takes pleasure in telling stories from which "the element of gravity is deliberately
excluded, thereby betraying a futile and irrational frame of mind known
as 'irony'" ("Age of Wisdom," 193).

Oscar Vincent, a bookseller and Latin scholar, is approached in a left-
bank Parisian brasserie by a time traveler belonging to the lost civilization of Badari. Conversing in Latin, the two men discover that the
Badarian has jumped forward some 8,000 years in time, thanks to a
modern version of the time machine, "a small lusterless white object
more or less ellipsoid in shape. A keyboard consisting of various buttons
and levers projects from it and thus appears to constitute the entire
mechanism" ("Time out of Mind," 13). But there is a witness to their
meeting, a Pergolian (Pergolia does not yet exist but will exist in the
distant future) who has been entrusted with the mission of undertaking
a voyage of exploration into the past, making use of a time machine
similar to that of the Badarian. With this machine the Pergolian travels
further back in time to visit the Badarian civilization, where he marvels
at its beauty, good fortune, prosperity, and the wisdom of its small
population.

Henceforth, the two time travelers spend their time in each other's
epoch with stops in the twentieth century—which will prove to be a
convenient battleground—assassinating and playing countless tricks on
each other. Their trips back and forth in time give rise to unusual situations and the Badarian suggests that they attempt to extend the radius
of action of their machines, which heretofore has been limited to 20,000
years. "Think of the day when we shall be able to reach epochs even further back in time," he exclaims, "to arrive at the era of the appearance of
life on Earth! To correct, yes, correct the blunders of Nature! . . . It will
be granted to us *to be the cause of what has been achieved*" ("Time out of
Mind," 34–35).

But the Pergolian does not at the moment have such great ambitions
and instead provokes a murderous combat between Pergolians and
Badarians in a Parisian nightclub, even as the poor bookshop owner, in a
marvelously comic harangue, begs them to stop:

Is this murderous combat really necessary here and now, when we happen to be at peace and on the road to perfection? . . . What characterizes
this century is science, and scientific subtlety. In Physics, for instance, we
have just demonstrated that all the laws established before our time were
false; furthermore, we have also established that no such laws could exist
and that the behavior of the Universe was just a matter of chance. We do
not know how to create matter, but we have recently discovered how to
destroy it. In the science known as Mathematics we have succeeded in
bestowing a definition on the indefinable, based precisely on its property
of being indefinable, which reveals a quite exceptional ingenuity. ("Time
out of Mind," 37)

The bookseller then concludes, in an ironic passage reminiscent of the
work of the seventeenth-century *philosophe* Montesquieu:

Perhaps it is under the heading of Metaphysics that our research has been
crowned with the most striking success. In this realm, having recognized
that God and the World are equally inconceivable, we have built up
more or less every possible theory to combine these two entities. I only
have time to mention them briefly: we first of all asserted that God had
created the World; next, that the World was created by itself; after that,
that these two incomprehensibles were fused in one, which was likewise
incomprehensible; next, that only the one or the other existed; and finally, making the most audacious intellectual effort in the whole of our history, we rounded off the series by conceiving a world that had created
God. We have a genius, I tell you, a positive genius for expediency and
improvisation when it comes to elements that escape us! ("Time out of
Mind," 38)

The unfortunate bookseller learns that the battle cannot be stopped
because it has been fixed in time to take place in his epoch. The passage
describing the battle itself—with its brain straining twists and turns—
as seen by a twentieth-century spectator from the doorway of a Parisian
cabaret, is among the most extraordinary in the science fiction genre:

It was an unimaginable scuffle. I was surrounded by clouds of shooting
stars that changed into warriors clothed alternately in a variety of cos-
tumes. I realized that each soldier, to deceive his enemy, was making
feints into the past and into the future. . . . I saw the Badarians disappear
all of a sudden, then come back armed with flints and dressed in
bearskins. They had probably made a small mistake and gone a little too
far back in time. At this spectacle the Pergolians vanished in a puff of
smoke and reappeared armed with long spears, drawn up in a square

which I took to be the Macedonian phalanx. Whereupon the Badarian unit changed into a motorized squadron. . . . Strange-looking corpses littered the floor of the night club, rose to their feet, cursed one another in outlandish tongues, wrestled together, shrank in size, grew bigger, turned into monsters, foetuses, groups of atoms. Ray clashed with ray, wave with wave. Rivers of blood flowed through the room, coagulated and disappeared in the same moment. ("Time out of Mind," 39–40)

Although the battle is rather complicated, the outcome is very simple: "The Badarian race has disappeared; the Pergolian race has taken its place. . . . The Pergolians have become the Badarians; but in the course of history the Badarians have in their turn become the Pergolians. They are at one and the same time our ancestors, ourselves and our descendants, we are their forefathers and also their offspring" ("Time out of Mind," 41).

And the story begins again where it ended, in the same spot in which it began, when the book dealer picks up one of the time machines dropped by a Badarian/Pergolian and goes back 12 hours in time to the evening before. "I was about to pass through this infernal night all over again and, since I was going to relive it in every detail, *inevitably, when dawn came, I would pick up the machine and press the button.* I would then go back in time and again relive this night . . . again and again, for ever and ever. My little gesture had fettered me to this fatal cycle" ("Time out of Mind," 42).

The science fiction theme of change brought about by some new scientific innovation is developed in "Time out of Mind" by means of a time machine that traps a man in a hallucinatory sphere of multiple identity and alternate worlds. In "Le règne des sages" ("The Age of Wisdom"), the change is effected by uncontrolled technology that produces a cataclysm. The opening lines of the story announce ultimate catastrophe to the reader familiar with Boulle's weltanschauung: "The world was at last governed by wisdom and learning. After centuries of error, reason and science had prevailed over ancient superstitions. Mankind had ceased to be at loggerheads. Religion and politics had lost their interest. Geographical frontiers had been abolished. Tribes, nations, sects and religions had gradually disappeared and fused into increasingly larger organisms" ("Age of Wisdom," 187). Now, in the twenty-first century, there remained only two human groups, two schools of science into which the world's population was divided. The first of the two, known as the "Corpuscular," or "Electronic," school, teaches that everything in the universe is composed of small elements called "electrons," and the second, known as the "Undulist," or "Vibratory," school, "maintains on the contrary that waves are the essence of the world and denounces the electron as an illusion created by the imperfection of our senses and measuring instruments" ("Age of Wisdom," 187). But both agree on one thing, the necessity for scientific discoveries to contribute to the welfare and happiness of humanity.

Both parties, each according to its own view of the universe, invent at the same time a new method to improve the human condition by overcoming the extremes of climate—lowering the temperature of the equatorial zones and raising that of the polar regions—so as to create gentle even temperatures throughout the world. The Electronic school decides to use 50 giant transformer-transmitter units to draw off all the surplus heat in the equatorial regions and 50 receiver-transformer groups in the arctic and antarctic regions to receive this warmth. The Vibratory party, on the other hand, prefers to release the waves necessary to transfer the excess heat of the equatorial regions into energy waves, transmit these waves to the cold regions, and then bring about the opposite transformation on their arrival. Both put their plans into action simultaneously, causing the temperature at the equator to go down to minus $40°$ centigrade and the temperature at the North Pole to rise at the same time to $40°$ centigrade. The North Pole becomes too hot and the tropics freeze; everything and everyone there dies. "They all perished . . . and the Earth was rid of several million inhabitants—albeit the least interesting from the scientific point of view" ("Age of Wisdom," 205).

Like "The Age of Wisdom," "Le parfait robot" ("The Perfect Robot") presents both sides of the science fiction theme of the wonders of science—the benefits of its marvelous gadgets and inventions and the disasters that ensue when change runs wild. Here, however, the emphasis is placed on the relationship between man and his creation. In a significant breakthrough in the field of cybernetics,[4] a scientist succeeds in creating a perfect robot, one that is even capable of engendering other robots, thus demonstrating that, since the scientist's role could now be eliminated, "the creative spirit should consequently be attributed to the robot considered as an eternal entity" ("The Perfect Robot," 90). But the scientist's detractors say that his robots are still not human because they lack some indefinable characteristics. After years of experiments in which he attempts to make them more human, the scientist comes up with a surprising solution. He discovers that his machines can be made to act and think exactly like human beings provided that they are endowed with certain human qualities they have heretofore lacked: an artistic sense, a sense of humor, and above all the ability to make mistakes.

A particularly outrageous illustration of the science fiction theme of the wonders of science is the story "Le poids d'un sonnet" (The weight of a sonnet). The protagonist of the story, Boulle's alter ego, referred to as "my friend Bourdon" ("Poids," 89), loves enigmas; he is happy only when he has mysteries to solve and spends a good part of his time seeking them out. The rest of the time he uses his vivid imagination and his unusual insight to search out their hidden truths. Bourdon does not restrict his inquiries to any special field, since he is interested in the problem per se, and brings the same enthusiasm to perfecting bridge strategy, to deciphering ancient languages, and to understanding the mysteries of the universe. His choice of subject is influenced only by the depth and difficulty of the problem to be solved.

When the story opens, Bourdon is faced with a most difficult problem. His friend, the writer Valette, died at his desk from an attack of apoplexy just as he was about to light a cigar. The match fell from his hand and burned the papers on his desk; a glass plate saved the desk from destruction. Valette's secretary tells Bourdon that the author had been working on a new work and that the fire had certainly deprived the world of a masterpiece. For, she adds, no one will ever know his last thoughts, a challenge Bourdon cannot resist: "I felt the thrill that runs through the lover of enigmas when he senses the possibility of a marvelous discovery" ("Poids," 82). And so Bourdon decides to bring forth a literary masterpiece from a small pile of ashes. After all, he remarks, "The foremost philosophers tell us that nothingness is an illusion. In the most complete void imaginable, Bergson said, our CONSCIOUSNESS still remains. Here, there is even more, for we also have ashes. This precious matter is still impregnated with thought" ("Poids," 83).

The preposterous methods used by Bourdon to reconstruct the burned work—described in 10 pages that read like the step-by-step decoding of a secret document—are presented with the precision of a scientific experiment. Bourdon succeeds in rescuing the work, a sonnet bearing the name of a fossil "The Pithecanthrope," worthy, of course, only of the ashes to which it has accidentally been consigned. But, Bourdon concludes, the quality of the work does not matter; it is only the solving of the enigma that is important.

Besides, one may ask, is the weight of a comma, the weight of a sonnet, any less worthy of examination than the weight of the human soul?[5] An amusing article in the *New York Times* of 4 January 1994 tells of an

English physicist, whose humor is identical to Boulle's, who proposes applying advanced laboratory techniques to measuring the soul and putting some theological ideas to a quantitative test. Dr. David Jones suggests that by attaching "piezoelectric transducers, inertial-navigation accelerometers," and other instruments to a dying person, it should be possible to measure the direction, velocity, and "spin" of the soul—spin being a quantum property of subnuclear particles—as it leaves the body. The change in body weight would reveal the soul's mass.[6]

In many cases, it is impossible to separate science fiction from science fantasy, since both contain elements of the fantastic in varying degrees. The fine distinction between them is that "science fiction deals with improbable possibilities, fantasy with plausible impossibilities" (Aldiss and Wingrove, 8). The last of the *Contes de l'absurde*, "L'hallucination" ("The Hallucination"), takes the reader into a nightmarish fantasy world reminiscent of those found in Poe's horror stories. The story opens as the head of Police Services checks out instruments of torture, making sure everything is perfectly prepared, before stepping aside so that his assistants can carry out his orders. He then enters his office. A click in his brain coincides with the first sounds of the torture. At that precise moment a hallucination begins. He is in Dante's hell, where he watches in horror as the demons torture the damned using methods not far removed from those being employed in the adjoining room. Finally, in the last circle of hell, the demon with the wild boar's tusk spreads his wings and moves silently toward his desk. The spell is broken by the sound of his assistant's voice informing him that the prisoner will talk. When he hears this familiar, reassuring voice, he is suddenly freed of the anguish that tortured him. The hallucination vanishes; the evil spirits are conjured. He feels the intense relief one has on awakening from a nightmare, and exclaims: "When I think that sitting right here in my chair, I could have mistaken this office for Hell and my own men for demons!" ("Hallucination," 287).

Pierre Boulle has often been taxed with insensibility because he refuses to pronounce any *mot d'auteur.* One of the rare occasions on which he abandons his role of impartial observer is in "E = mc² ou le roman d'une idée," the title story of his second collection of short stories, $E=mc^2$,[7] when his usual classical restraint gives way to a cry of anguish: "Why, in this world, do the noblest enterprises often end in a result which does not reflect the purity of the initial intention and is even in direct opposition to the generous principles that inspired them? Why does so much love give rise to so much disorder?" ("E=mc²," 350–51).

To illustrate this inevitable perversion of noble intentions, Boulle fashions a science fiction tale based on a very cruel reversal of Albert Einstein's formula $E = mc^2$. This formula, which for Boulle represents the cornerstone of the modern world, shows the theoretical equivalence of matter and energy. It establishes the proposition that "each particle of matter is equivalent to a quantity of energy equal to the product of its mass by the square of the speed of light" ("$E = mc^2$," 288). Insight into the properties of matter was provided in 1938 when the scientist Otto Hahn—Otto Hans in Boulle's story—split and reduced the nucleus of the heaviest atom, the uranium atom, to its simplest elements.

To convince humanity of the fact that energy and matter are transformable, one into the other, Einstein, in Boulle's story, proposes to the American president that a scientist create matter from cosmic energy. He "must collect, condense the invisible energy that is scattered all over the world and dissipated every second to no profit and . . . transform it into matter, into solid, visible, palpable matter that every human being can see and touch" ("$E = mc^2$," 312).

The president reprimands him for interest in a purely theoretical project when war is imminent. What is essential, he reminds Einstein, is to create energy from matter; to destroy matter by means of a rapid chain reaction in order to produce a powerful weapon. The idea of creating such a bomb fills Einstein and his fellow scientists with horror. "The struggle we have been waging for years now, Mr. President," Einstein says, "is an intellectual struggle; the struggle of truth against error and lies. A conflict of this sort requires spiritual weapons: the possibility of giving the world palpable proof of a great truth" ("$E = mc^2$," 326).

Boulle's story now progresses from scientific fact to science fiction. One of the scientists does succeed in creating a synthetic atom of uranium by collecting and condensing cosmic energy scattered throughout the universe, and concludes that "one or several atoms having been created by cosmic energy, a reaction known as 'chain' must build up spontaneously through the action of natural forces. From those first elements other atoms must be born and their number increased, following a geometric progression" ("$E = mc^2$," 335). The scientists then decide to perform the experiment in a Japanese city where Einstein had been received graciously in the past, as a gesture of friendship designed to show the constructive nature of science. And so they release "the energy condenser" ("$E = mc^2$," 344), a slender leaf of synthetic uranium that floats down over the city of Hiroshima. Multiplying as the result of a chain reaction, the uranium falls thicker and thicker and the chain reaction gives no sign of slowing down, creating a disaster the scientists had not anticipated. Hiroshima is buried and disappears, not beneath volcanic ash, like Pompeii, but beneath a shining blanket of uranium.

The second story in the collection $E=mc^2$, "L'amour et la pesanteur" ("Love and Gravity")—a story dedicated by Boulle to "science fiction fanatics"[8] and written long before the first Sputnik was launched—is an amusing account of a wedding night aboard a satellite in orbit. The captain of the crew explains to the newlyweds the scientific principles governing weightlessness in space: "Every time you push against an obstacle it sends you backwards in the opposite direction to the push. It can be up, down, to the right or to the left; for there is no gravity to hold you in check" ("Love and Gravity," 259). In space action = reaction, he adds, thereby setting the stage for the difficulties, described in comic detail, that are encountered by the partners as they attempt to consummate their marriage. The astronauts conclude glumly that a satellite may be perfect for scientific observations, but, "for love, it's just a complete, plain washout" ("Love and Gravity," 274).

Boulle may have been the first to raise the question facetiously, but 35 years later scientific speculation becomes scientific topicality, as demonstrated in a *New York Times* article, which announces that "one of the most delicate and secret topics of the space age is beginning to go public, at least a bit: sex in space."[9] The witty article could have been written by Pierre Boulle himself: "Astronauts duck questions about it and officials of the National Aeronautics and Space Administration often wince at its mention, fearful of appearing to *condone eroticism in the heavens at public expense.* . . . Though experts say intercourse itself has yet to occur on a spaceship of any kind. . . . romantic couplings are all but inevitable. As a result . . . a number of serious issues of science, engineering, medicine and psychology need to be openly discussed" (Broad, C9; italics added).

"Les Luniens" ("The Lunians") is written in the form of the science fiction cum philosophical tale that satirizes contemporary problems. It is in this genre that present-day social, political, and technological developments can be exaggerated and extrapolated to underscore what the author perceives to be dangerous—in this case, the stupidity of the cold war rivalry between the United States and the Soviet Union. When the story opens, the American contingent of Operation Moon, which had landed secretly on the blind side of the moon, reports to the president of the United States and the Secret Interplanetary Committee that living creatures exist there. They have given the name of Lunians to these inhabitants, for whom they feel an instinctive liking. At the same time, Comrade Zarkoff, commander of Soviet Secret Confidential Services, has also received reports from his space contingent that creatures with human characteristics are living on the Moon. They are "not only reasonable and industrious creatures, but also kindly, amiable, affable, peace loving, amenable, cultured, and quick-witted" ("Lunians," 152).

The reports sent back to their respective countries by the moon explorers provide commentary on the economic, social, and philosophical ideas of the two cultures. The American account of the Lunian's intellectual probity, the absence of preconceived ideas, and their self-criticism constitutes a satiric reference to the trumped-up show trials in Russia. The Russian report, which finds that the method of government of the Lunians is the "Lunian fulfillment of a divine doctrine. . . . contained in a book they call the Bible" ("Lunians," 162), mocks American hubris. Unfortunately, admiration, communication, and peaceful coexistence disappear with disastrous consequences when each side discovers that those they call Lunians are "ordinary, horrible men from Earth!" ("Lunians," 174). The leaders of the two contingents, unable to stand the shock of discovery, fall dead, and the rest of the explorers take refuge in their respective camps to await instructions from Earth. After two days all are told to evacuate the moon and keep moving for 40 days in outer space to undergo a period of "delunization" before being permitted back on Earth. In addition, they are to take measures to blow up the Moon immediately following their departure, since it has become too important a strategic point to be allowed to subsist after the enemy has set foot on it. And so it was done!

The Moon may have been destroyed, but its disappearance had no serious consequences. On the contrary, writes Boulle, ever the gentle satirist, there was a positive side. Dangerous tides disappeared, poets ceased "indulging in sickening comparisons on the brilliance of the heavenly body. Madmen became less mad, wise men wiser. The quiet of the night was no longer disturbed by dogs baying. And last but not least . . . women's characters improved, became more equable, and were no longer subject, as in the past, to unpredictable moods" ("Lunians," 175).

The last story of the anthology $E = mc^2$, "Le miracle" ("The Miracle"), is not science fiction. Science, however, is not absent, for the story centers around the conflict between science and religion, a conflict that not only has preoccupied both scientists and philosophers for centuries but also constitutes an important theme in Boulle's work. Despite his own professed lack of belief (Interview, 19 November 1990), Boulle's Catholic education is evident in much of his work.

The protagonist of the story, Father Montoire, has a great reputation. He is admired by his parishioners, and the ecclesiastical authorities regard him as a future pillar of the Church. The priest rejects the so-called conflict between faith and reason, insisting that "the most materialistic science, concerned exclusively with facts and experimentation, is now obliged to recognize its inability to understand everything and explain everything. . . . Modern science has been forced to admit the possibility of exceptions to laws it had believed to be immutable" ("Miracle," 54–55). One day a woman comes to see Father Montoire, sent by his friend, the nonbeliever Doctor Faivre, who has failed to convince her that her son's blindness is incurable. Unable to refuse the poor woman's request, Father Montoire touches the blind man's eyes and then turns away, tormented by his inability to help this suffering individual. But a miracle has taken place, the young man can see. The priest consults Doctor Faivre, who assures him that the man's organs of sight had been destroyed and that only a miracle could have restored his vision. Convinced that a miracle has indeed taken place, the doctor embraces religion. The priest, however, keeps seeking a rational explanation for the "miracle," in which he alone is unable to believe.

Boulle's irony dictated the choice of the title of his third collection of stories, for the very notion of charity is conspicuously absent from these *Histoires charitables* (Charitable stories).[10] The adjectives *grinçantes* (grating) or *farfelues* (eccentric) more aptly describe these stories in which we find the absurd humor characteristic of Boulle's other works. They are not all equally successful, but all skillfully blend logic and absurdity, caricature and reality, fantasy and plausibility. One, in fact, "Le compte à rebours" (The countdown), is not even a story but a rather mediocre, mildly amusing poem on the death of Pope Jean XXIII. Another "charitable" story, "L'arme diabolique" ("The Diabolical Weapon"), is a model of absurd logic in which a committee of military men that has been formed to establish policy in the event of war concludes that atomic weapons make war impossible and the military consequently useless. For this reason, they resolve, these diabolical weapons must be banned, not to prevent destruction but to permit conventional warfare.

Two of the *Histoires charitables* reveal certain of Boulle's ideas on the novelist and the art of the novel. The first, "Histoire du bon petit écrivain" (The story of the good little writer),[11] censures the mediocre writer who wastes whatever talent he may have in his search for fame and deplores at the same time the lack of appreciation accorded the good writer who devotes himself to his craft and refuses to court popular opinion. The good writer in Boulle's story finally achieves posthumously the fame he had always deserved by turning himself into a human torch, a gesture that brings him the success and glory denied him during his lifetime.

In "L'homme qui ramassait les épingles" ("The Man Who Picked Up Pins"), an amazing tour de force, Boulle states his concept of the novel obliquely, ridiculing at the same time several famous proverbs he finds meretricious. How idiotic, according to Boulle, are the adages "There is no such thing as a small saving" ("Pins," 46) and "Genius nowhere reveals itself so much as in minute attention to detail" ("Pins," 47). They are the stock-in-trade of certain philosophers who quibble over the slightest detail or writers of similar ilk who are constantly on the lookout for minutiae. Boulle points out here the absurdity of the cautionary tale, which poisoned the youth of his generation, about an impoverished young man who goes to see a wealthy banker to apply for a job. He is turned down definitively, but, as he makes his way towards the door, he stops suddenly with his eyes fixed on the floor, bends down, carefully picks up a pin, and sticks it in the lapel of his coat. The banker, who has been observing him, is moved by this gesture, calls him back, takes him on as his partner, and gives him his daughter in marriage together with half his fortune. The admiration for this act is based on the dogma that "the entire importance of the world derives from insignificant details, and the moral of which teaches that the mind will raise itself to the essential truths by fastening exclusively on these minute details" ("Pins," 46). On the contrary, Boulle maintains, "genius consists in scorning small details and fastening straight away on the essential" ("Pins," 49), for "happiness, in point of fact, derives from *big* things, like vast wealth, like genius, like anything else substantial" ("Pins," 50).

Boulle scorns this young man as a false example of economy and virtue and shows that such a man is destined not for success but for a lifetime of crime, including the despicable invention of the new novel, which "attaches no importance to the subject, [and] starts working from material details like words, full-stops and commas" ("Pins," 49). Boulle here criticizes the new novel—with its repeated descriptions of objects in minute detail—so contrary to his own insistence on the importance of plot.

"Le saint énigmatique" ("The Enigmatic Saint") is Boulle's favorite "charitable" story, perhaps because it is the most gruesome and also perhaps because of its diabolical surprise ending, the most effective in all of his short fiction. A stranger comes into a leper colony where, to the astonishment of all, he kisses without disgust and without fear of contagion all of the lepers, including even the most completely disfigured among them. The prior of the colony warns the stranger of the dangers he runs, but to his remonstrances the enigmatic saint replies with the rhetorical question: "Are not all men brothers?" ("Saint," 107).

The lepers wonder whether he is a repentant sinner or a messenger sent by God to transform their infernal region into a kingdom of love. "He may be a saint," one of the lepers concurs, but "I am prompted to look for explanations, and I am usually inclined to think that self-interest is a powerful motive of human behavior, even for a saint" ("Saint," 125–26). Indeed, self-interest rules the world; there is no charity, there are no saints, Boulle again reminds us in the dénouement. After the stranger has kissed all of the lepers, he is found to be carrying the plague, the black death, which is "a hundred times more contagious, a thousand times more terrible than leprosy" ("Saint," 138). "Leprosy kills slowly" ("Saint," 101), but the plague is a scourge that kills in five terrible days of indescribable agony.

At the center of the *Histoires charitables* is "L'homme qui haïssait les machines" ("The Man Who Hated Machines"), an amusing, amoral science fiction story depicting the conflict between technology and human ingenuity. The narrator of the story, who speaks for Boulle, is fascinated when he sees a man in a bookstore who avoids the electronic beam that opens the door to the store. "Those who know me," he writes, "who are aware of the horror roused in me by the conventional, and the raptures, on the other hand, into which I am plunged by the slightest odd behavior on the part of my fellow humans, will realize how tickled I was by this prelude and with what fervor I started avidly watching each of his gestures" ("Machines," 207). And so he speaks to the strange man in whom he senses a kindred spirit; a feeling that is confirmed when he sees in the man's eyes "the disturbing, fleeting little gleam . . . the heavenly seal with which the Angel of Oddity marks certain privileged creatures" ("Machines," 208). The man tells him that he is infuriated by the stupidity of machines and feels rewarded when he succeeds in exposing their ineptitude to the world. His goal is to win the conflict between creative intelligence and automatism.

In an effort to explain the origins of his hatred for machines, the man tells the narrator the story of his life. He had an extensive scientific education, after which he worked in a power station, where he sabotaged a turbine so that it finally exploded. He describes the scene in an offhand manner: "Twenty tons of thundering whirling matter then went hurtling through the roof of the factory and landed half a mile away, reducing some houses to rubble, [and] preserving, encrusted in the débris, a few fragments of the mechanic's brain" ("Machines," 215). To his great surprise, he was tried for his "brilliant achievement" and confined to a mental hospital after having described on the witness stand the feeling of unrest that took hold of him whenever he encountered mechanical ineptitude, an unrest that had gradually grown into an intolerable anguish. During his confinement, he sabotaged several of the appliances in the hospital, where at the same time he became a mathematical expert, hoping to match wits eventually with a calculator. Unable to find employment after his release from the hospital, he became a mercenary in the Central American war between the states of Balaka and Béléké, where he succeeded in outwitting an ultramodern antiaircraft gun, causing it to fire on itself. He killed his good friend in the process—but c'est la vie.

At the end of the war, the man who hated machines met an eccentric wealthy man who became his patron and pitted his protégé against a giant calculator. Boulle notes that such a contest actually took place in 1924, adding that, after he completed his story, a fresh contest took place between a human calculator and an electronic machine ("Machines," 231). In 1992, 27 years after Boulle wrote his story, science fiction again became reality when a mathematician named Tinsley played 39 checker games against the Canadian-designed Chinook computer in a tournament for the world title, before finally triumphing with a 4–2 victory.[12]

Boulle's hero also won his match against the machine, and his patron decided to replace it with a more sophisticated machine, an electronic computer, to further test his protégé. During the fantastic contest that then took place, the man who hated machines succumbed to the magnetic power of the electronic computer and had to undergo brain surgery. The patron subsequently died. We understand that it was at the hands of our hero, who was at last free to exact his revenge on the computer. He took the detested machine apart and then put it together again to achieve absolute, perfect, ideal disorder, making it incapable of adding even 1 + 1. He then invites the narrator to view his handiwork and, in a wonderful takeoff on Descartes's famous proposition, he remarks: "I cheat, therefore I think, and that is one of my incontestable advantages" ("Machines," 241). But he has gloated too soon. His destruction of the machine was a Pyrrhic victory, for he, too, has become inhuman in the process. His obsession has turned him into an automaton that is no more capable than the broken machine of calculating 1 + 1.

What is absurd, both in the real world and one bathed in myth and fantasy, according to Pierre Boulle, is the discrepancy between the way things are and the way we perceive them; the divorce between what is and what might be. There is no great contrast between the stories that take place on Earth in the first part of *Quia absurdum (sur la terre comme au ciel)* (*Because It Is Absurd {On Earth as in Heaven}*), and in heaven in the second part—although the heavenly stories are more imaginative—for all of them are steeped in an atmosphere of absurdity that invites the reader to reexamine former beliefs and convictions. Each of the stories relies on a supernatural or highly improbable event to bring about a surprising revelation. All are wry, witty, and ironic; they reflect Boulle's ingenuity and his diabolical logic of insanity. One, "The Duck Blind,"[13] is different from all of Boulle's short stories, for it is autobiographical. It is the sole account of his early years before the publication of the *L'îlon* in 1990. Strangely, too, this is the only work that might be viewed in the existentialist sense of the absurd, since it describes the author's wait year after year in a duck blind for ducks that will no more appear than Beckett's Godot.

In "Son dernier combat" ("His Last Battle"), the author imagines the meeting, 20 years after the capture of Berlin, of a former Nazi henchman and Hitler, who fled his bunker and has been living as a farmer in a remote area in the Andes with Eva Braun. The Nazi learns that Herr Wallj, Hitler's pseudonym, has terrible nightmares that disturb his otherwise idyllic existence and believes that the Führer is consumed with remorse for having killed 6 million Jews. Not at all! One morning, in a remarkable surprise ending, Hitler appears smiling as if relieved of a great weight. He explains his joy in a monstrous confidence: "I've won. . . . The last battle. It has been hard, but I've come out victorious. . . . It took me a long time to make my decision, but it is final. I have driven all hatred out of my heart. . . . The Jews—I have forgiven them."[14]

"Le plombier" ("The Plumber"), another story with roots in World War II, tells of a German captain who finds himself in an awkward position because the machines for torturing his prisoners—two bathtubs, one for ice water and the other for boiling water—no longer function, and he is obliged to wait patiently as the only plumber in the area slowly repairs them. Since the plumber does not understand that these are instruments of torture, it is natural that he finds that these people with their extravagant needs behave like the nouveau riche.

"Interférences" ("Interferences") is centered around one of Boulle's favorite themes—one that also ties together the stories of the *Histoires perfides* of 1976—that a single miscalculation inevitably causes even the best laid plans to go awry. A man, who is being deceived by the wife he adores, puts his affairs in order so that after his death she can have sufficient means to live happily with her penniless lover. Then he hires a killer and arranges to have himself murdered so that it will appear that he was victim of an attack, for his life insurance does not cover suicide. The night the hired killer murders him, the lover, who has also decided to kill him, is privy to the murder committed by the hired assassin. Fearful of being accused, the lover makes the murder appear to be a suicide, thereby thwarting the plans of the dead man and leaving the woman without the resources to support them.

In the second part of the collection, Boulle relocates the absurd to heaven, construed in both the religious and spatial senses of the word. In the first story, "Quand le serpent échoua" ("When the Serpent Failed"), Boulle uses a comic technique that consists of imagining alternate scenarios for historical events or well-known tales. The story takes place on a newly formed planet in a remote stellar system, where Eve decides to obey God's law and not taste the forbidden fruit. And that is the great flaw in the system of the All Powerful, not to have foreseen that an Eve could, of her own free will, refuse the forbidden fruit from the Tree of the Knowledge of Good and Evil ("Serpent," 91). The serpent is nonplused and speechless, for he has played this role before on all the 3 billion planets already created in the universe, and it is the first time he has been denied. He threatens Eve with death, but she replies that he is mistaken, for she has eaten the fruit of the Tree of Life and has gained life eternal. Instead, she tells him, he is the one who will die, because he has eaten the forbidden fruit as he was demonstrating its wonders to her. Then the woman seizes a stick and kills the serpent with one blow, exclaiming, "You see now, I was right" ("Serpent," 94).

The Lord is perplexed. He cannot punish her and drive her from Paradise, since her only crime was to obey his command. The situation is serious enough for him to consult the Holy Computer, Omega, with whom He discusses the implications of this absurd situation—including the question of free will—for "woman is perfectly free to sin or not to sin" ("Serpent," 101), and He could not have foreseen the possibility of her obeying His command. The discussion continues with Boulle's usual logical development of the absurd: "If these creatures persist in obeying, they will, first of all, remain ignorant of the knowledge of good and evil and, secondly, they will be immortal" ("Serpent," 101–2). In vain does the demon—the serpent is dead but the spirit of evil that inhabited it is eternal—renew his efforts to tempt her, first in the guise of a wounded peacock and then of the most charming animals on Earth. The Holy Computer decides to appeal to Adam, using logic and reason rather than seduction. But the man finally says: "You weary me. I'm not accustomed to reasoning. I obey" ("Serpent," 111).

Omega states that the situation is becoming catastrophic. The people, immortal, will increase to billions of creatures ignorant of good and evil, they will invade and wipe out the inhabitants on all the other planets in the universe, and "all that because that silly goose refuses to eat an apple!" ("Serpent," 117). It is then decided that the Second Person, the Son, is the only one qualified to get them out of this dilemma. To his Father's objections, the Son replies: "If original sin is not committed on this planet, I shall find myself in a situation at least as critical as yours. . . . No sin, no atonement. No atonement, no Redeemer" ("Serpent," 119). And so one evening the woman sees a youth of supernatural beauty rather than a disgusting serpent appear at the foot of the Tree of Knowledge of Good and Evil, filling her with a strange emotion; she eats the heavenly fruit, and her companion follows suit. They are, of course, "driven out of Paradise and forced to earn their bread by the sweat of their brow. If, eventually, they committed almost as many follies and crimes as they would have committed in their state of innocence, according to the Computer's dream, that was not important from the cosmic point of view for, since they had become mortal and subject to divine justice, the Lord could always exterminate them when their excesses became dangerous to the harmony and conscience of the Universe" ("Serpent," 124), Boulle concludes ironically.

"Les lieux saints" ("The Holy Places"), a slight tale, also stars Omega, the Holy Computer, who "delights in statistics and claims that only numbers possess true eloquence" ("Holy Places," 136). He has computed the number of murders committed in the name of religion and for this reason orders an angelic commando to destroy in a night in Jerusalem all traces of Christian, Moslem, and Jewish religions.

Boulle revisits the heavens of space exploration in the final and most successful story of the collection, a science fiction tale titled "Le coeur et la galaxie" ("The Heart and the Galaxy"). Here, as in *L'univers ondoyant,* he explores the possibility of the existence of extraterrestrial civilizations, anticipating NASA's ambitious program to monitor the heavens for possible radio signals from outer space. NASA spent 20 years and more than $50 million to develop sophisticated digital receivers, capable of listening to tens of millions of frequencies at a time, on the assumption that somewhere among the half-trillion stars in the Milky Way galaxy life may have begun and evolved to a state of technical sophistication comparable with or superior to that on Earth.[15]

Boulle's story centers around this search for extraterrestrial life. It takes place in a lunar observatory, where, after 10 years of silence, four people hear signals coming from 40,000 light years away in the past; it is a mysterious message from a distant world written in the binary alphabet.[16] The message is repeated at regular intervals; it is certainly *the Message* ("Galaxy," 188), revealing perhaps the great mystery of the universe. In an unprecedented display of planetary unity, all of the scholars of the world join forces to decode it, their research funded by billions from all of their countries. After two years, the message is deciphered. In a typical turnabout, Boulle mocks his own belief in the existence of extraterrestrial civilizations, for the message is a ridiculous sample of a Miss Lonely-Hearts column: "Is there in the Galaxy a heart generous and compassionate enough to take pity on and heal the wounds of an unhappy woman shamefully deceived and bruised by life? A heart overflowing with tenderness" ("Galaxy," 190).

The six stories of *Histoires perfides* (*The Marvelous Palace and Other Stories*) are supposedly told to a writer desperately in need of inspiration by a vaguely Oriental centenarian, perhaps "an incarnation of the devil,"[17] who, the writer reveals, resembles him like a brother. He seeks out the company of this old man on evenings when, "driven to despair by the frightful clichés the Western world offers the professional story teller, sickened by the banality of personal experience and having taken a meritorious but imprudent oath never again to make use of such subjectivity in my writing, I would willingly abandon my soul to the Demon in exchange for an original idea" (Introduction, 9). The "perfidious" stories are clearly the work of an author who loves the bizarre for its own sake and takes perverse pleasure in certain curious, at times sinister, adventures. Strange, disquieting occurrences are for Boulle the essence of storytelling; "the finest sentiments never beget good literature" ("La grâce royale" ["The Royal Pardon"], 14).

The centenarian resembles the author in an even more significant way. He is a self-professed priest of the religion of doubt, a religion that Boulle, by his own admission, embraces.[18] The old man explains the tenets of his strange faith: "In the matter of religion, every firm belief is presumption. No being is yet wise enough to be able to judge of the existence or nonexistence of a God or a cosmic consciousness. If one must, one can nourish the hope that the humanity of a few thousand years hence will arrive at a modest probability on this subject. But for the present, humility and wisdom consist in recognizing our inability and taking refuge in Doubt. That is Doubt's essential element" ("Le palais merveilleux" [The marvelous place], 53).

The stories in this collection, which take place in the mysterious Kingdom of Shandong, are centered around variations on a recurring theme in Boulle's work—the inevitable corruption of noble sentiments. In the first story, "The Royal Pardon," it is maternal love, "a virtue much honored in the Kingdom of Shandong" (13), according to the sly old wizard, who starts his story by describing the interview the queen of Shandong granted him when he was young.

At that time he was a lawyer defending a young man who was most likely innocent of the crime of which he was accused, and he pleaded with the queen to pardon his client and spare his life. He felt he was winning his case, when the telephone rang. As the queen spoke on the telephone, he sensed that the atmosphere had grown ominous and that the queen, who was favorable to his case a moment before, had changed her mind. She asked him strange questions about the age and state of health of his client, and then astonished the lawyer by refusing to pardon the young man. The queen's secretary explained what had motivated her decision: her 20-year-old son, exactly the same age as his client, was suffering from a terminal cardiac ailment and his only chance of survival was a heart transplant. Since most citizens of the paradise of Shandong died of advanced old age, the queen saw in the young man to be executed a unique opportunity to save her son's life.

"Providentially," the night before the execution, a young man, a single man without living parents, was savagely attacked at knife point. And, by a strange coincidence, it was none other than the condemned man's mother who called the police that night. A neighbor, awakened with a start by the victim's cry, rushed toward the cottage, which he reached at almost the same time as the police. Everything happened as if the mother's call preceded rather than followed the murder. But, says the old man, his "eyes glowing like a cat's" ("Pardon," 23), perhaps the mother had a premonition of the attempt to be made. It was possibly "an act of Providence, for it allowed specialists to find a body still warm and to operate with the greatest chance of success. Doubtless one must see even there an example of maternal love carried to the extreme: a prayer so fervent, it obliged Providence to manifest itself" ("Pardon," 33).

The second story of the collection, "The Marvelous Palace," which gives its name to the title of the English translation, confirms that it is not only noble sentiments that are inevitably corrupted but also original, imaginative endeavors that are doomed to destruction, a recurring theme in Boulle's work: "When men of energy are stirred by creative passions, they always carry to a happy conclusion the task they've set themselves, no matter how arduous and difficult; they triumph over every obstacle and refuse to be discouraged by the criticism leveled against them. . . . [But] once they've attained their ultimate aim, the work brought to a close by virtue of their intelligence, their labor, their desperate drive, is revealed to be useless and derisory because one little detail has escaped their genius" ("Palace," 37).

The Marvelous Palace is the name given to a collective undertaking carried out by the ministers of the Kingdom of Shandong. The principal promoter is the minister of statistics, whose idea it is to centralize executions at a single point in the kingdom and to create there an exemplary new center designed to spare the condemned all pain other than the supreme punishment. To counter critics of the proposal, the ministers use the justification of "murder considered as a fine art" ("Palace," 52), declaring that it would be scandalous not to apply it to lawful capital punishment. Boulle describes in an offhand manner the great ingenuity applied to effecting capital punishment, or "legal murder," which he also castigates in *Le bourreau* (*The Executioner*). Again and again, Boulle forces us to examine beliefs and customs we had taken for granted, not by denouncing them but by merely presenting them in all their absurdity.

But the Marvelous Palace is never used. Everything has been foreseen except for one detail—the death penalty is abolished. The vagaries of storytelling require, however, that it be restored in the following story, "Les lois" ("The Laws"), the tragic tale of Sinar, the most beautiful and virtuous dancer of the corps de ballet of the royal dancers of Shandong. When the narrator left Shandong for a brief period, Sinar was at the peak of her career; when he returns after a few months, she is shut up in a dark prison and condemned to death for having had an abortion. Because Shandong has a declining birth rate, voluntary abortion is punished by death. The taking of life in the name of saving life is a paradox that delights an author whose work is devoted to the uncovering of such absurdity; absurdity on a par with the bombing of abortion clinics and the murdering of doctors under the banner of "right to life."

Sinar was not believed when she claimed that she had been raped by one of the noblest princes of Shandong. Because rape was the only extenuating circumstance for abortion, the ministers thought she had lied. Here, as in all of the stories, the irony of the situation swells to grotesque proportions.[19] When the minister of doubt visits Sinar in prison, she attempts to seduce him and, failing that, turns to her jailer, a depraved monster, for her only hope of salvation is to become pregnant. A woman who is carrying a human life is sacred in the eyes of the law in Shandong. Paradoxically, a pregnancy had been the cause of her ruin, and now it represents her only chance of saving herself. The minister of doubt finds her reasoning logically irreproachable, and he cannot fault her seduction of the jailer, since, like his creator, he has always been inclined to forgive many a transgression in the name of logic. Three months later, he is sent to the prison to announce Sinar's pardon—the man who had raped her confessed the truth on his deathbed. She collapses and dies on receiving the news. She had been able to bear the horror of what she had done to save her life, but not its absurdity.

Absurdity is absent in the eminently logical story "Les limites de l'endurance" ("The Limits of Endurance") that follows. Written in the French classical tradition of reason, logic, and restraint, it even echoes one of the maxims of La Rochefoucauld: "we always have strength enough to endure the troubles of others" (La Rochefoucauld, 37). It is the story of a woman in her 60s who is afflicted with an incurable, dreadfully painful disease. She cries that she can no longer bear the pain and begs for help to put an end to her agony, but her husband refuses because "a life is sacred and under no circumstances should be cut short by a human hand under the pretext of pity" ("Endurance," 101). She fills the house with unbearable shrieks, lamentations, and pleas, but her husband remains adamant in his refusal and retires to his garden. Soon afterward the wife dies, her suicide finally abetted by her husband, who confesses that he left a vial of pills within her reach. Why then did he suddenly become capable of such an act? His servant reveals that a foreign doctor had told the man that the patient needed fresh air and demanded that the windows of her bedroom be opened night and day. The garden was now filled with her cries; his last refuge had been denied him. "If she hadn't died in the night," the servant continues, "I believe that he would have gone mad" ("Endurance," 117). "Endurance of pain has its limits" ("Endurance," 121), Boulle concludes.

The next story, "Service compassion" ("Compassion Service"), illustrates another aphorism, in this case that goodness and compassion disappear when self-interest is involved. The old pseudonarrator, who plays the role of observer in the other stories, here is one of the protagonists. He first tells about his early years as an unsuccessful lawyer and the reasons for his decision to give up the practice of law to become a minister of the religion of doubt. Poor and depressed and contemplating suicide, he sees an advertisement for an association of volunteers—headed by a saintly man who goes by the name of M. Vincent—who are ready at all hours to receive the calls of persons in despair to console them and to help them recover their joie de vivre. He, in turn, becomes part of the family of Compassion Service in order to help others as he, himself, was helped. One of his callers is a woman who tells him repeatedly about the cruelty of her husband. As she speaks more and more frequently of suicide, he feels that he lacks the experience required to deal with her problems and asks M. Vincent to listen in on her next phone call and advise him. When they hang up the phone, the older man says: "My young friend, to give you useful counsel is impossible. An odd case such as one meets with every now and then. I can do nothing for her. . . . It is my wife" ("Service," 155).

The last of the *Histoires perfides,* titled "L'angélique monsieur Edyh" ("The Angelic Monsieur Edyh"), does not illustrate a maxim as do the others. It is a science fiction story, a variation on Robert Louis Stevenson's *The Strange Case of Dr. Jekyll and Mr. Hyde,* a story that centers around the idea of the double, the doppelgänger, the alter ego, or second self. This idea haunts the history of literature, for it goes straight to the heart of a fundamental process of fiction making: the imagining of another, the projections of one's hopes, fears, and inclinations onto an imaginary other. Unlike Stevenson, who split the bestial id and the civilized superego into two personas, showing the superiority of the latter over the former, Boulle, always the devil's advocate, transforms the story to show the destructive power of the civilized superego.

The story told by the old man is about a friend of his—whom he calls Jekyll for purposes of the plot—a scientist who had studied physics, biology, and the application of these disciplines to medical research. His friend was also interested in literature and was particularly stuck by the passage in Stevenson's work in which Dr. Jekyll reflects on the first time he swallowed the potion he had compounded and gave birth to the evil Mr. Hyde: "Had I approached my discovery in a more noble spirit, had I risked the experiment while under the empire of generous or pious aspirations, all must have been otherwise, and from these agonies of death and birth I had come forth an angel instead of a fiend" ("Monsieur Edyh," 157).

The scientist in Boulle's story discovers the composition of a drink that makes it possible to divide a human being into two, physically and morally, and to isolate in one of the parts all the good or all the evil, whose complex intermingling in himself tormented him just as it had disturbed Stevenson's hero. He decides to embark on the venture only after he is certain that his orientation is toward the good, and begins to lead an exemplary and edifying life, even separating himself from his fiancée and postponing their marriage. Only then does he perform the experiment that gives birth to the angelic M. Edyh, who promptly proceeds to give away a substantial portion of Jekyll's money. Soon the scientist is unable to control Edyh, who is summoned forth without need of a potion whenever he comes into any contact with an unfortunate person. Thus, a chance meeting with a leper brings forth M. Edyh; he marries her, abandoning Jekyll's fiancée, and uses what remains of the scientist's money to build her a palace.

M. Edyh is pleased with all the good he has done until one day he comes upon Jekyll's former fiancée, now clearly the most unhappy creature in the world. And so he turns back into Jekyll, whom he has ruined with his generosity. When he sees all the misery he has caused, Edyh poisons himself, never suspecting that he is also doing away with Jekyll. The good scientist dies, his fiancée goes mad and has to be shut up in an asylum, and the leper dies of loneliness, sorrow, and despair. Unquestioning good has created destruction and havoc, a most disturbing paradox.

The torment occasioned by the divided passions of the human soul has been at the center of much of Pierre Boulle's work. At times, as in "The Angelic Monsieur Edyh," the author presents the problem in terms of an external influence, a magic potion. At others—and we find this in many of his novels—he presents the problem in psychological terms, showing how an idée fixe can transform a decent man into a monomaniacal monster. Finally—and this is the case in the philosophical tale *A nous deux, Satan!* (Now, let's fight it out, Satan!)—the author uses the religious symbols of God and Satan to present the same struggle for control of the human spirit.

The protagonist of the novella *A nous deux, Satan!* is the Abbé Jerville, an exorcist in a town in the Auvergne. He is said to be the incarnation of Good, as Satan is the spirit of Evil. One day he is called upon to exorcise a young boy who shows irrefutable signs that the devil has gained possession of both his body and his soul. After checking carefully for psychiatric explanations, the exorcist decides to intervene. Using methods recommended by the Church, documented very carefully and completely by Boulle,[20] he forces the devil to free his victim; but Satan avenges this defeat by taking possession of the Abbé himself. The third round in the struggle between Good and Evil belongs to the Abbé, who immolates himself on a burning pyre in order to destroy at the same time the Evil that has taken over his body and soul.

In keeping with his refusal to form a conclusion, however, Boulle does not assure us that Satan has burned with his victim. We know that the good priest is dead, but has Satan not escaped to possess another individual, another group, another civilization? The ending of the work suggests what is clearly expressed at the end of Camus's novel *La peste,* when the plague has finally disappeared from the city of Oran. The narrator reminds the joyous survivors that the victory is only temporary, for the plague bacillus is never completely destroyed; it merely lies dormant, only to surge forth at a future date to destroy its new victims.

In a second cautionary tale, *The Executioner,* Boulle turns his irony on the legalistic refinements of capital punishment, effectively emphasizing the mindless, impersonal cruelties that can be inflicted by custom or group psychology. The narrative is told by an old Chinese doctor who bears a striking resemblance to the minister of doubt of the *Histoires perfides* and thus to the author. It takes place in the magical city of Yin-Yang in the province of Li-Kang, twin to the marvelous Kingdom of Shandong, both of which are modeled on the remote Chinese mountain military post at Pin-Ku-Yin of Boulle's wartime séjour described in *My Own River Kwai.*[21]

The executioner Chong is charged with the odd crime of murdering his condemned clients by administering to them a very special dose of poison 15 minutes before beheading them, in order, it seems, to spare them the prolonged ritual murder prescribed by law. The authorities, outraged and bewildered, sentence him to torture and death in a courtroom marvelously adorned with banners inscribed with the maxims of the greatest sages, carefully chosen to suit the occasion: "It is an abominable crime to disturb the established order"; "Thou shalt not kill"; "Whosoever takes another man's life is as cruel as the tiger of the forests, and a thousand times more contemptible, for the tiger does not know what he is doing."[22]

The motives behind Chong's actions are made apparent during his trial, the full account of which occupies the major part of the novella. Chong, the son of the chief executioner, was to follow his father in his profession, but, after botching an execution, he was forced to flee his province. He lived miserably in exile for 10 years. A year before his return, his last employer gave him a bottle of precious poison to spare

him, in case of infection, the agony of the plague that was rampant in
the region. Chong was so miserable that he decided to use the poison on
himself, his wretched, blind consort, and his dog. He tried it out on the
dog first and saw it die without suffering. When he compared the dog's
peaceful death with the horrible death of the man whose execution he
had mishandled, he felt that it was his duty to expiate his clumsiness and
the horror of the execution by allowing the condemned to die as the dog
had died. Chong and his consort, two "pilgrims" (*Executioner,* 104), set
out on foot for the province of Li-Kang along the dreadful roads of
Yunnan, carrying the poison, which seems to them to be a magic philter
enabling them to triumph over every ordeal to come. They endure
poverty, hunger, thirst, fatigue, and fear. They are captured by brigands
and nearly devoured by rats, "tests" from which they, like Hercules from
his labors, always emerge victorious. Their trials and suffering, like those
of the reformed heroin addict Butler in *The Virtues of Hell,*[23] although
endured for unusual reasons, demonstrate Boulle's contention that it is
the quest that is important—not the motivation or the end result.

The spurious arguments of the plaintiffs in the trial permit Boulle to
set forth—always indirectly without authorial comment—a comprehensive indictment of the insanities of society. The families of the seven victims maintain that, by preventing the condemned men from carrying
out their role in the ceremony and showing a manly attitude, the executioner caused their families to lose face. Then the priests of the three
cults present their arguments. The Buddhist priest explains that in
depriving the convicted man of his final quarter of an hour of existence,
the executioner no doubt prevented him from performing an act of charity, thereby forcing his soul to be reincarnated in the body of an inferior
animal. The Taoist priest maintains that the executioner denied the condemned men a quarter of an hour that was particularly propitious to
mystical emotions and profound meditation. The Confucian sage presents the only reasonable argument; he says merely that Chong had violated the ritual. The most telling accusation, however, is that of the
attorney general, who states that "from the strictly juridical point of
view Chong had on seven occasions violated the Chinese law that forbids
killing" (*Executioner,* 160). And so, the executioner is executed for having
executed in a "non-executionally" approved manner. "Off with their
heads," cries the Red Queen in a parallel wonderland.

The narrator in Boulle's third exemplary tale, *Les coulisses du ciel*
(*Trouble in Paradise*), is a scientist, an astrophysicist who speaks for the
author. "Everything fills me with wonder," he states, "but nothing

surprises me. If I'm never surprised it's because I'm engaged in a profession where daily occurrences can be so strange that . . . [nothing can] be considered an astounding phenomenon."[24] The occurrences are indeed strange in this amusing parable about the paradox of three-part monotheism, which begins with a séance, proceeds to a series of sectarian discourses, and concludes with a second Assumption.

In the opening scene, the Holy Spirit escorts Mary from Heaven to France; their mission is to negotiate a consensus among the various factions of the faithful whose disputes are to blame for the rivalry between Father and Son. God the Father is about to be supplanted by God the Son because the trend of Christian theology, which favors Jesus as the preeminent person of the Trinity, has upset the balance of power. Boulle has the Spirit—using the open-minded astrophysicist as a medium—present a synopsis of 20 centuries of councils, synods, heresies, and schisms that have led to the present trouble in Paradise, trouble that, in fact, does not seem to differ from the normal, everyday filial rebellion against parental authority. First the Son became insolent and openly defiant of the Almighty. Then they began to quarrel, each intent on imposing his own will. When the Father separated the good souls from the bad and punished the latter mercilessly, the Son countered by preaching his message of love, based on forgiveness of sins and pardon of offenses. "Didn't I redeem them once and for all?" he would shout (*Paradise*, 32–33).

The philosophical astrophysicist-medium, the only one to have anticipated the controversy, remarks: "I had always marveled at the feat engineered by the Christians when they united in a single entity two personalities as dissimilar as the Father and Son. In their haste to synthesize everything, they prodded the councils into forging a monstrous amalgam, which was bound to explode one day. Think about it . . . on the one hand absolute power, harsh discipline bordering on cruelty, a tyrannical impulse; on the other, infinite goodness, mercy, forgiveness of sins, humility. That such a monster should devour itself doesn't astonish me at all" (*Paradise,* 60).

Mary has tired of the childish disputes between Father and Son and begins to neglect her mission, concentrating instead on taking steps to assume her rightful place in the celestial hierarchy. When Mary is questioned about what she believes to be her true essence, she replies that in her heart and conscience she's not sure of anything. She mentions that when the so-called palaver started about her virginity, she found it indecent and wanted to rebel, but as the debate continued, she, herself,

began to have doubts. Finally, when Pope Pius IX decreed that she was
not only immaculate but innocent of sin as well, it became an article of
faith and she felt obligated to hush her rebellious inner voice (*Paradise,*
34). Boulle treats the matter with tongue in cheek, but a recent newspaper article makes it apparent that the questions raised here are still being
actively debated: "For nearly two millennia the Virgin Mary has been
venerated as the exemplar of feminine perfection. A holy enigma, she
was both mother and virgin. She spoke with angels. She was the consort
of God. . . . Such is the picture of the perfect mother and woman paint-
ed by 2,000 years of church tradition and popular piety. Now, however,
some prominent church leaders are not only challenging the Virgin
Birth, as others have for hundreds of years, but are arguing that the
church's Mary is a myth that contributes mightily to the oppression of
women."[25]

As theologians of all faiths—including, ironically, a Marxist philosopher—discuss the dispute between Father and Son, the Virgin Mary
takes center stage. Adored by all, she embarks on a political career and
is elected president of France. The recognition she is now receiving as a
political leader and a woman and the prayers offered in Church to her
celestial image provide her with the solution to the dispute in Heaven.
In a low-cut designer dress, adorned with a Legion of Honor ribbon, she
ascends to heaven, her second Assumption even more glorious and spectacular than the first. There she is hailed as Goddess, the only Goddess,
since "the Father, the Son, and the Holy Spirit are mere demigods—really thirds of a god—and the proof is that the three of them had to get
together to make the one, which is only an illusion anyway" (*Paradise,*
185).

The power of illusion to distort our perceptions and control our lives
is the basic idea underlying all of Boulle's short stories and philosophical tales. In the religious sphere, illusions have given birth to the myths
that purportedly justify the incalculable numbers of murders committed throughout the centuries in the name of religion. Illusions also are
responsible for so-called miracles, as well as for theological hairsplitting
over perceptions of the Immaculate Conception and the Trinity. The
illusions that spring from belief in the miracles promised by science, the
new religion, are similarly shattered. Boulle's stories show that while
space travel may transport humanity to the heavens, it provides there
merely a new terrain for conflict and warfare; and the marvelous discoveries that promise to control our environment succeed only in
destroying that environment. The mechanical wonders created by

science undermine our ability to think and feel, and one of the greatest of all scientific discoveries, Albert Einstein's formula $E = mc^2$, leads to the most terrible weapon ever created. Our so-called noble sentiments—mother love, conjugal love, charity, and respect for life—are merely elegant camouflage for crimes sanctioned by society. Yet, what would seem to be a pitiless indictment of all human beliefs and practices is mitigated by Boulle's refusal to judge or condemn and, ironically, by the true "Christian charity" of this nonbeliever.

Chapter Six

The Novelist and the
Art of the Novel

Pierre Boulle was determined to conceal the person behind the writer; he never discussed his emotions or the intimate details of his private life. His constraint not only stemmed from an innate sense of modesty and reserve but also reflected his belief that, rather than the life of the writer, it is his or her writing that is important.[1] Boulle was never reticent, however, about discussing his work, particularly his ideas on the theory and practice of the novel.

The most—or perhaps the only important element in any novel—in Boulle's opinion, is the story it tells. In "The Man Who Picked Up Pins," he ridicules the writers of the new novel who compare the writer to a camera, replacing plot with enumerations of the objects that come into the camera's view. A camera may indeed objectively film external reality, but, as Boulle demonstrates in *The Photographer,* the photographer makes a choice in this reality, a choice that tells its own story. Without a plot, Boulle remarks, whatever one may call it, there is no novel.

The first step for Boulle in writing a novel is to find the idea that will set the creative process in motion. But, where do the ideas come from, what is their source? Sometimes, Boulle states, an idea can spring from a news headline that catches his eye. For example, his fancy was struck when he read that, in the course of a demonstration of the precision of their instruments, the scientists of the laboratory at New Brunswick weighed a comma ("Poids," 89). This headline developed into the story "Le poids d'un sonnet." An idea can also grow out of an article in a journal, as was the case with the description in the *Armed Forces Journal* of 15 February 1971 of the electronic sensors dropped by American aircraft over Vietnamese supply routes, the starting point for *Ears of the Jungle.* *Planet of the Apes* came out of a visit to a zoo, *The Good Leviathan* from a newspaper account of an oil spill that polluted the beaches of Brittany. The account of the rescue of a Dutch girl from the Japanese by a Malay family during World War II and her subsequent inability to readjust to life in Europe supplied the background for *The Test.* Other works stem from abstract concepts: absurdity in *Not the Glory* and *The Bridge over the River Kwai;* the correspondence between good and evil in *The Other Side of the Coin*. Still others, like *L'univers ondoyant* and *Garden on the Moon,* reflect certain of the author's basic preoccupations, like cosmology and space exploration. While it is impossible to pinpoint precisely the source of all of his ideas, the most important factor, according to Boulle, is chance. He adds that if he were a conceited person, he might even say inspiration (Interview, 28 November 1990).

Once in possession of an idea, Boulle elaborates on it. Here, his chief concern, he explains, is to distinguish himself from others. With this in view, he visualizes a priori a peculiar situation that, by human standards, is utterly improbable (*Executioner,* 8–9). As a result, we find in his work a fanatic Nazi spy who dies for England (*Not the Glory*); an honorable public prosecutor who condemns to death a man he knows to be innocent (*Face of a Hero*); an English colonel who, blinded by his belief in his racial superiority and determined to prove it to the Japanese during World War II, constructs the very bridge that will carry the Japanese army to fight against the British in India (*The Bridge over the River Kwai*).

The obstacle to this approach is that the characters in the novels must almost always be modeled on those one might find in real life. "But how am I to take my characters from real life," he wonders, "when I endow them with absurd reasoning? How am I to choose them from among us, since they have to behave in every circumstance like puppets?" (*Executioner,* 9). The difficulty then is to make the reader suspend disbelief as he reconciles the seemingly average protagonist with his bizarre behavior. This is perhaps facilitated by the fact that Boulle's characters are two-dimensional. There is no psychological analysis of these characters, no probing into their subconscious that would allow the reader to identify with them or question their motives and reactions. "As for me," Boulle remarks, "I try to find actions that express the essence of the characters. That is the basic attribute of the novelist. I do not like long speeches or analyses. And the psychology of the character must be revealed by his behavior. It seems to me that in almost all of my novels I followed that line of conduct" (Interview, 19 November 1990). In consequence, the reader, separated from the characters by the same distance as that provided by objective newspaper reports, can read about them dispassionately and concentrate on the details of the plot.

Above all, Boulle continues, "I do my best to achieve an effect of surprise, and when several possibilities of this sort come up for consideration, I naturally choose the one that presents the most outrageous and

most inconceivable absurdity. Then, taking into account that my readers, after all, are human beings, I strive to endow the situation with a
deceptive appearance of rationality and bring it to life by means of a false
logical sequence that perfidiously tends to make it acceptable. I thus
achieve a further factitious effect: the effect of contrast" (*Executioner,* 9).

Two of Boulle's novels, *Le malheur des uns . . .* (One man's joy [is
another man's sorrow]) and *La baleine des Malouines* (*The Whale of the
Victoria Cross*), although considered by the author to be minor works,[2]
exemplify the techniques used in the major works; the birth and elabo-
ration of an idea, the development of and variations on major themes,
the lack of psychological analysis, the emphasis on action, the reconcilia-
tion of reality and absurdity and of strangeness and simplicity, and, finally, the masterful integration of topical issues into the narratives.

In the preface to *Le malheur des uns . . .* , Boulle provides insight into
the genesis of an idea. The revelation that would alter the course of the
life of Boulle's protagonist, Alexander Shark, the powerful director of the
International Corporation of Malayan Heveas, was the result of the juxtaposition of two apparently unrelated news items he read in 1982. The
first described the threat posed to the future of the planet by the thin-
ning of the ozone layer that protects us from the harmful rays of the sun.
This danger, in and of itself, did not alarm Shark, who was basically optimistic about the future of the Earth. What had captured his attention
was the reason for the destruction of this protective layer. It was not
caused by any planetary cataclysm but by a series of apparently insignificant factors; the enemy that was eating away the protective ozone layer
was the chlorofluorocarbon, or CFC, produced by ordinary household
appliances. This gas is contained in vaporizers and atomizers, in refriger-
ators, synthetic foams, car seats, and polystyrene wrapping materials,
and it accounts for an annual production of several million tons of deadly material. Shark was struck by the curious disproportion here between
cause and effect.

It was then that the "god of chance"[3] who rules the world placed
another article, with no relationship to the first, before Shark's eyes. It
was about a sickness that had been puzzling doctors and epidemiologists
for more than a year, particularly in America; a sexually transmitted disease just baptized with the initials AIDS (Acquired Immune Deficiency
Syndrome); a disease that was going to have worldwide repercussions.
The article gave alarming statistics on the exponential growth of the disease, deplored the fact that there was as yet no vaccine for it and no rem-
edy to cure it, and concluded by stating that at the moment the most

effective method to protect oneself from this terrible scourge was by the use of condoms. "Stark stared at the last word. Only the light in his eyes gave evidence of the stream of intuitions, deductions, and inductions that suddenly flooded his mind. He was stunned, dumbfounded by an idea that had just been born . . . [and] filled with wonder at the possibilities of which his feverish brain had just caught a glimpse" (*Malheur,* 12–13).

When Shark described his epiphany to his friend, the psychiatrist Dr. George, the latter explained that there was a hidden relationship between the two articles, despite the seeming absence of any link between them. This relationship could be explained by the discrepancy between cause and effect stressed in each article. He added that several of his patients had experienced similar flashes of inspiration—particularly writers searching for an original theme—which would appear suddenly in all their splendor following the connecting of two or three insignificant incidents with no apparent link among them. The trivial cause Shark read about in the first article was the emission of gasses from vaporizers used to kill insects or dispense perfume; the far-reaching results constituted a threat to humanity owing to the deterioration of the atmosphere. The trivial object in the second article was a simple rubber article weighing less than a few grams; the incalculable consequences could be the salvation of humanity.

Anticipating the incredible possibilities offered by his findings, Shark takes sweeping measures to corner the market on latex, buying controlling shares in the depressed rubber industry, obtaining land concessions from the government of Malaya, and controlling the market on the centrifuges that are indispensable to the production of latex for condoms. He also orchestrates a media campaign to generate fear of the disease and make the public aware of the necessity of using the only defense available against it. His company prospers as the AIDS epidemic becomes a worldwide catastrophe, even as scientists throughout the world work to stop the plague.

Fearing that scientists may soon find either a vaccine to prevent AIDS or a cure for the disease, Shark stops at nothing to halt their progress. The actions of this monomaniac, as he sabotages the work of scientists, killing them when he bombs their laboratories, stem from the idée fixe that possesses him, governing all his thoughts and actions. He belongs to the family of fanatics like Colonel Nicholson (*The Bridge over the River Kwai*), Gaur (*The Photographer*), Cousin (*A Noble Profession*), Butler (*The Virtues of Hell*), Trouvère (*L'énergie du désespoir*), Blondeau (*Mirrors of the*

Sun), Mortimer (*Le professeur Mortimer*), and the historical figure emperor Frederick II (*L'étrange croisade de l'empereur Frédéric II*); he is "one of those people who give themselves without qualms to ensure the success of their enterprise, completely oblivious to the appalling consequences that can result from their actions. The souls of such creatures are shielded from remorse, which cannot breach the armor protecting their conscience. Such individuals are legion" (*Malheur,* 166).

To put an end to the somewhat tedious account of Shark's spiraling successes and vile machinations, Boulle had recourse to an arbitrary dénouement brought about by the intervention of a deus ex machina, here the AIDS virus. Shark's beloved son, Alain, who has been in Malaya learning about the different aspects of the rubber industry, becomes infected with AIDS, a tragedy described with the simplicity that characterizes Boulle's style: "It happened a little while after his arrival in Malaya. A gathering of young assistants, bachelors. An outing to Kuala Lumpur, which they take two or three times a month; the only distraction from the work and isolation of plantation life. A dinner washed down with plenty of wine. Then a visit to an illegal brothel. . . . He had drunk a good deal of whisky contrary to his usual practice. He forgot to take the precautions that are indispensable nowadays" (*Malheur,* 224).

The account of Alain's infection reminds the reader that there is no sexuality in all of Boulle's work. His two principal novels demonstrate this in different ways. It is completely absent from *The Bridge over the River Kwai,* where there are only men of all ages and nationalities whose sole interest is to stay alive; and it is ridiculed in *Planet of the Apes* when Ulysse Mérou, "one of the kings of creation," embarks "like a peacock around the gorgeous Nova on the love display" (*Planet,* 105). But it is not only sex that is absent—none of the basic human activities take place in Boulle's work. His characters do not eat, sleep, enjoy family life, or have religious or political convictions. They have professions, but are rarely seen exercising these professions. This is because they are there solely to convey the idea at the heart of the novel.

At the end of *Le Malheur des uns . . . ,* one man's sorrow ceases to be another man's joy. Shark has triumphed over every obstacle and attained his ultimate aim, but his desperate drive and labor have become useless and derisory because one little detail has escaped his genius[4]—the possibility of ever having need of the potential cures for AIDS that have disappeared in the laboratories he destroyed.

Shark's defeat reflects a change that took place in Boulle's novels after 1981. The protagonists of the early novels experience the personal victory of never recognizing defeat, of refusing to admit the madness of a totally illogical project. Nicholson saves his bridge from destruction, and Gaur takes the photograph of a lifetime—the death agony of the assassination of the French president. Cousin dies with his heroic self-image intact, faithful in death to his fanciful vision of himself as the heroic spy sacrificing his life for his country. The public prosecutor Berthier convinces himself that he is the defender of the poor, and the reformed drug addict Butler creates a true chemical miracle, the purest heroin ever distilled. The protagonists of the later novels, however, like Shark, are punished for their crimes.[5] Trouvère's establishment for the production of psychic energy is destroyed, Blondeau's solar-power installation is an ecological disaster, and Professor Mortimer's cure for cancer fails to save his beloved dog. These dénouements, which are more in keeping with traditional novels—and particularly with the detective novel in which evil doers are punished for their crimes—do not reflect Boulle's characteristic irony, which posits vice as its own reward.

Still, whether victorious or defeated, Boulle's characters fail to move the reader. Raskolnikov (*Crime and Punishment*) commits a heinous crime—he savagely murders an old woman—but the reader shares his guilt and torment. Emma Bovary is stupid and vain, unfaithful to the devoted husband she ruins, but we feel her desperate frustration as did her creator. "Madame Bovary, c'est moi," Flaubert declared, but there is not a single reader of Boulle's works who could identify with his protagonists any more than one might with Voltaire's Candide. Boulle's characters are neither real nor persuasive. Even Colonel Nicholson is nothing more than a military rank, a curiosity and not a person; his uniform is empty. Boulle cannot be faulted for this, however, since the sole function of the characters in his novels is to further the plot; plot is the province of this master storyteller. The reader is interested only in what will happen, not why it happens. Here, as in all of Boulle's novels, with the exception of the autobiographical *S.O.P.H.I.A.* (the only novel, too, in which we find a three-dimensional, believable protagonist), there is a single story line—with no subplots—often the singleminded pursuit of a goal dictated by a consuming passion.

The mood of *Le malheur des uns . . .* is unremittingly somber and grim, unlike the light, humorous tone of *The Whale of the Victoria Cross.* Together, these works are representative of both sides of the novelist; on the one hand there is the moralist concerned with the plight of human beings torn between conflicting passions, and on the other the comic philosopher who finds wicked humor in even the most serious matters.

The pessimism of the vision of human nature in thrall to the demon of perversity is balanced by tolerant amusement, a dry, ironic view of humanity that will, in the end, muddle through.

The Whale of the Victoria Cross—where Boulle again gives an affectionate portrayal of English eccentricity, as he did in his first novel, *Not the Glory*—was inspired by a speech made in May 1982 during the Falklands conflict by Prince Philip, Duke of Edinburgh and president of the World Wildlife Fund, in which he said: "Attention! On radar, cetaceans often look like submarines."[6] This message is delivered to the admiral of the fleet as the British flotilla, carrying some 5,000 men, courses along the South Atlantic "to recapture some remote islands" (*Whale,* 153), the Falklands. The admiral explains the instructions it contains, euphemistically designated as information, to the other officers. It is essentially an example of Hobson's choice—an apparent freedom to reject or accept something offered when in actual fact no such freedom exists. The communication means in effect that if the radar signals a strange object, if the submarine detection system picks it up 200 feet below, the ship's captain is welcome to drop his depth charges on it, for that is his duty. But if after this the mangled body of a whale floats to the surface, the English public, passionate in its love for animals, will be outraged. If, on the other hand, he heeds the advice of the Duke of Edinburgh and makes sure there is no whale before launching his depth charges "for fear of harming some poor creature of the deep, a glorious link in nature's chain," and is torpedoed, then he is guilty of negligence and subject to court-martial (*Whale,* 11).

As Clark, the captain of the destroyer *Daring,* an escort vessel fitted for antisubmarine warfare, is poring over the bulletin he has just received, the radar picks up an unidentified object several miles away. Clark cannot make up his mind; he is worried about the whales, yet at the same time tempted to open fire. Fortunately, he waits, and two blue whales surface. As the crew watches, a pack of killer whales attack the blue whales. The attack, in the course of which the male is killed and the female injured, is described in detail, as the members of the crew watch in horror and beg their captain to intercede to save the surviving blue whale. Boulle gleefully contrasts the Englishman's love of animals with the pragmatism of the Americans, who at the first radar signal would have pumped "a bellyful of lead" into the whale. "And a great shame it would have been, for she's really a beautiful animal. . . . After all, perhaps it's no crime to be a bit eccentric" (*Whale,* 127).

The crew of the *Daring* fires upon the killer whales and destroys them. While the novel up to this point is realistic, and although there have been innumerable accounts of the astounding intelligence of dolphins and whales, the remainder of the novel moves off into the realm of magical realism. From then on the grateful blue whale, like the lion in the story of the Roman slave Androclès,[7] becomes the protector of her human benefactors. The sailors begin to feel that the whale is their mascot, a guardian angel shielding them from the ocean's perils. In keeping with an important theme in Boulle's work—humanity's inherent need for religious belief—the whale, like the giant tanker in *The Good Leviathan,* becomes the center of religious fervor. The Christian admiral wonders whether the whale was sent from heaven or hell, and a Hindu sailor writes to his family in Nepal that it may be one of the God Vishnu's incarnations, "the most impressive: the initial one, the *matse-avatar* . . . [which represents Vishnu the Preserver] as a man from the waist up; below the waist is something resembling a large fish, which people nowadays take for an awkwardly drawn whale" (*Whale,* 148–49).

The blue whale helps to break the monotony of the long voyage by her antics, twisting, turning, and rolling. She also performs heroic deeds; she intercepts mines designed to explode on exposure to a magnetic field and rescues on her back sailors thrown from a torpedoed vessel. Finally, she throws herself in the path of a target-seeking torpedo, "an act of heroism that rarely occurs in the human community, but never . . . in the animal kingdom" (*Whale,* 179). The admiral's recommendation that the whale be awarded the most coveted decoration of all, the Victoria Cross, demonstrates once again Boulle's contention that there is no limit to the outrageous.

Typically, women exist only in the margins of *Le malheur des uns . . .* and *The Whale of the Victoria Cross,* unless the anthropomorphic whale can be considered to be a member of the female sex. The whale here, like the chimpanzee Zira in *Planet of the Apes,* is a thinking female, while the human female Nova in the latter novel is a devoted, passive animal. The women in Boulle's work, and this is the exception to the topicality of his literary production, are barely realized sketches. Rather than characters, they are more like notes accumulated by the author with a view to projected fictional characters. Perhaps this has occurred because Boulle's novels explore what have always been traditional male provinces, such as war, foreign intrigue, adventure, cosmology, space exploration, and scientific research. Boulle declined to discuss the virtual absence of women in his work, other than as background, commenting merely that this was just the way it seemed to work out.

He did, however, point out the presence of two strong women with character—Madame Ngha, supreme head of the North Vietnamese Intelligence Services in *Ears of the Jungle,* and Madame Bach, owner of the nuclear tanker in *The Good Leviathan*—while acknowledging at the same time that there is nothing to characterize them as female. They are merely embodiments of abstract intelligence (Interview, 19 November 1990). There is, however, one important difference between them and Boulle's male protagonists, for they are neither consumed by passion nor dominated by the demon of the perverse. All of their actions are pragmatic. Even more, both of these women possess the ability to turn every unexpected event to their advantage.

Mme Ngha first sabotages the American sensors to direct the B-52 bombing raids onto the Jarai's hunting grounds to provide game for the hungry tribesmen. She then arranges for the planes to drop their napalm to clear the way for farming plots and their defoliants to clear the jungle and prepare the terrain for the proposed postwar Ho Chi Minh Way. Similarly, it is Mme Bach, a leader in the world of industry and finance, who first conceived the idea of building a 600,000-ton oil tanker with nuclear propulsion. To secure publicity for the tanker, she exploits the so-called miraculous cure of the cripple and sets up a thermal establishment adjoining the tanker—as medically valid as the one created by Pagnol's famous Doctor Knock—to cater to those who come seeking a cure for their maladies. She also builds a hotel to accommodate those accompanying the sick and a pilgrim's village with consumer services and well-stocked, financially profitable stores.

Significantly, the only woman who exists as a living female entity in all of Boulle's work, albeit in the traditional role of victim, is Germaine Dassier, the wife of one of the French planters in the autobiographical novel *S.O.P.H.I.A.* Boulle expresses great sympathy for Germaine and the other colonial wives living in exile in an alien environment where their only function is to be waited on. Sophia took a dim view of the unproductive class represented by the planters' wives, fearing that the formation of small family groups would undermine the team spirit and disrupt the sense of corporate unity. Many wives had thus resigned themselves to the status of "warrior's plaything." A few others nevertheless tried to struggle. Still others lost all hope and adopted a permanent attitude of hostility.

Germaine belonged to the last group, but did her best to drown her resentment by thinking of the joy of her family's impending home leave. Her daily routine never varied. In the morning, she watched her husband dress hurriedly for the 4 o'clock roll call, and then went back to sleep. When he returned one hour later, they had tea and fruit, and then strolled up and down in the damp garden until daybreak. She saw him again for a moment or two when he came back for a hasty breakfast, and again at 2 o'clock for lunch. After the meal, utterly exhausted, he took a short siesta, and then left for the divisional office, where he worked until six or seven in the evening. During this time, Germaine's son would go for a walk with his nurse and she generally went back to her bedroom, laid down again, and dozed until the heat became unbearable. She then drenched herself with cold water and went downstairs to the living room, where she stayed until evening with nothing to do, picking up a novel she did not read, putting it down again, picking up some needlework that she gave up almost immediately, or tried to write a letter to her parents that she would tear up after a few lines. When her husband finally came home, he shaved and showered, drank a glass of whisky, had dinner with her, and then went to bed immediately. Boulle conveys through Germaine's words, gestures, and thoughts her desperate unhappiness.

Finally, after their home leave is deferred several times by the company, Germaine can no longer bear it and takes the decisive step of leaving her husband, Sophia, and Malaya. Maille meets Germaine by chance in Singapore, where he has gone to wait for his orders to report for duty in Indochina. She is there awaiting passage back to France. In the only romantic episode in Boulle's work, in an atypically sensual atmosphere, they spend a week together in a bungalow near the sea surrounded by palms and coconut trees, with a veranda that looks out onto the sea,[8] "the warm gentle sea of Malaya impregnated by the rivers and streams with the damp scent of the jungle and the diabolical smell of the durians—perfumes that mingled on the beach at night with the barely perceptible ripples reflecting the faint glow of the moon" (*S.O.P.H.I.A*, 233). All of their senses are stimulated in this tropical paradise.

They get up at dawn, and "by way of breakfast they bite into the saffron-yellow flesh of a mango or else into the white pulp of a mangosteen, its purple skin still permeated with the cool breath of night" (*S.O.P.H.I.A.*, 233). They go for walks along the beach and watch the Malay fishermen cast their nets, then they plunge into the shade of the palm groves, where they find a series of kampongs scattered among the trees. They drink milk straight from the coconuts dropped by the children who climb to the tops of the trees to gather them. In the evening, they make their way back to the coast.

> The sun gilded the tops of the coconut trees and deepened the glow of the red varnish protecting the carved timbers of the bungalow. They waited till darkness fell, then gleefully stripped off their clothes. They wallowed in the phosphorescent warmth of the sea, running their fingers through its myriad milky reflections. They swam far out, heedless of the sharks and jelly fish, until the ocean breeze wafted new scents to their nostrils and a colder water, reminding them of other, more distant seas, brought miraculous relief to their aching limbs. They stayed in for a long time without touching bottom. Malaya was no longer visible, apart from one or two bright dots on the coast and the pale nimbus around their own house that served as a guiding light for their return. (*S.O.P.H.I.A.*, 233–34)

The language throughout Boulle's autobiographical novel is very different from that of his other novels, for it is evocative, not narrative. Images are the language of poetic evocations, and it is only in Boulle's autobiographical works that we find a whole series of brilliant images that speak to all of the senses. The sights, sounds, and odors of Malaya, all of the sensations that Boulle experienced during his early years there and that provide the atmosphere for his novels set in Southeast Asia, are summoned forth throughout *S.O.P.H.I.A.:*

> But seen from the summit of Bukit Taggar, the Malayan countryside revealed a vast splendor seething with an infinity of colors and shadows. The jungle appeared as a whirling chaos, a bewildering mosaic of startling vegetation, in which the hues of various climates clashed in a fantastic pattern that resulted, paradoxically, in perfect harmony. On the hills in the foreground, which seemed within arm's reach, all the burnished gold and russet tints of the European autumn vied for light with the greens of giant bamboos, wild palms, and banana trees, encompassing here and there a vernal patch of pink or violet. A mist as white as snow shrouded the slope above a valley that had just been cooled by a local shower. A little farther off and higher up, the colors grew less vivid. Farther off still they merged into one another, blending with the shadows in the limpid atmosphere, until at last they were transformed, each by the miracle of its own particular metamorphosis, into the uniform blue of the mountain range. The plantation was invisible to the casual glance. The eye had to be directed downward to a lower level in order to perceive it

nestling at the bottom of a chasm: a dingy patch of monotonous regularity, which struck the eye mainly on account of the red roofs of the nearest Tamil village and the incongruous rectilinear contours that marked its boundary. (*S.O.P.H.I.A.*, 42–43)

Even more remarkable is the manner in which Boulle uses language to convey the absence of sound:

The silence of the plantation created a more intense sensation. The sun had just gone down. Not a single bird celebrated the end of the day. Not a single rustle stirred the unvarying features of the artificial forest, which seemed depopulated. The jungle was too far away for the sound of its incipient activity to reach the bungalow. The pale trunks of the nearest rubber trees formed a perfect oval at the foot of the terraced garden. The foliage, clearly outlined in the foreground, melted into the distance in a solid compact mass. This was the farthest horizon. The bungalow was not high enough to afford a view of the world beyond the boundaries of Sophia except at one point where a deep gap between two hills revealed a small luminous triangle standing out against the highest peaks of Malaya.

The last sign of life was the passage of the flying foxes. These were giant bats, almost as big as vultures, that made the same pilgrimage every evening. They would take wing far away, in the direction of the sea, fly over the plantation zone at dusk, then make off in search of food in the jungle. Their altitude varied according to the season and the wind, but they always materialized at the same hour with clockwork regularity. Within a few minutes the whole sky was dotted with them. On a calm day, like this evening, they flew over fairly high—not too high, however, to prevent Maille, startled by the sight of this sudden invasion, from noticing the contractions of their membranes folding and unfolding in a series of rhythmic beats. Each black speck looked like a mechanical toy operated by an invisible spring. The flight passed overhead in a slow, steady procession. (*S.O.P.H.I.A.*, 28)

Boulle gave free rein to the romantic side of his temperament in his bildungsroman, which, as is the nature of the genre, expresses the youthful emotions and spiritual development of the protagonist. And then, like Flaubert, he spent the rest of his life mastering his sensibilities. Rather than a novelist of description, atmosphere, sensations, and emotions, he became, as he described himself, "an illustrator of ideas, one who looks for easily verifiable scientific truths, or other subjects, and then presents them with utmost simplicity."[9] He does this by means of linear plots with two-dimensional characters to exemplify the ideas. Boulle's dry, laconic style, devoid of images but characterized by logical mathematical demonstrations, is admirably suited to the presentation of this cerebral universe, providing a perfect correspondence between content and form. In the beginning of each of Boulle's novels is the idea, and ideas are abstractions best expressed by abstract language.

Conclusion

Pierre Boulle's work is unique in French literature. There are few contemporary writers whose novels reflect in such faithful detail the spirit and structure of our time. Major historical events are presented throughout his literary production, from colonialism in Southeast Asia during the first half of the century, through the growth of nationalism and liberation movements, to the end of colonialism; from World War II in both Europe and Asia to the American and French phases of the war in Vietnam. It is not only the major historical events but also contemporary concerns and problems that emerge, among them ecology, medical research, and animal rights; the search for cures for cancer and for AIDS; the need for increasing sources of power and the search for alternate, nonpolluting forms of energy; the abuses that exist in the French judicial and educational systems; the magnificent conquests of science such as space exploration and artificial intelligence, as well as the creation of the atomic bomb with the concomitant malaise, discomfiture, and fear that the discoveries of science will eventually destroy the very civilization that created them.

Boulle's oeuvre, however, is much more than a reflection on the fate of the individual in the great political, social, and intellectual upheavals of the modern world. Eternal human preoccupations also figure prominently in his work, particularly the search for answers to the questions of where the universe comes from, where it is going, and how we got here, questions that were formerly the province of religion and that now have been appropriated by science. In his essay on cosmology, *L'univers ondoyant,* as well as in many of his novels and short stories, Boulle probes the secrets of the cosmos and of extraterrestrial life.

Boulle's affinity with several English-language novelists is evident in his work. In it we find the echoes of Somerset Maughm's exotic colonial settings, Joseph Conrad's view of the English gentlemen and his posing of adult moral questions in terms of adolescent heroic adventures, Kipling's glorification of the British soldier, H. G. Wells's pessimistic science fiction, Edgar Allan Poe's tales of horror, and, particularly, Robert Louis Stevenson's *Dr. Jekyll and Mr. Hyde,* in which the author personifies the concept of the double, the alter ego, or second self. This symbolic representation of the divided passions of the human soul is at the core of

Boulle's work as he uses it to demonstrate how an idée fixe can transform a decent man into a monomaniacal monster.

But, by the philosophic irony that suffuses his tales of adventure and
quixotic accomplishment—whether it be the building of a bridge over
the River Kwai or a spacecraft that will transport man to the moon—
Boulle shows that he still belongs to the nation of Voltaire. Many of his
novels and short stories exemplify La Rochefoucauld's cynical *Maximes*
and echo the false naïveté of Montesquieu's putative Persians in *Les lettres
persanes,* as they underline the absurdity of French customs and beliefs.
The tone and concept of Voltaire's *contes philosophiques,* in which characters and plots are used to set forth a vision of the world, find expression
in Boulle's fiction, as does the eighteenth-century philosophical debate
about the efficacy of religion as a moral discipline.

Boulle's irony is always impersonal. He is a moralist in the seventeenth-century sense of the word, one who observes human behavior
with bemused objectivity and who notes his observations with a certain
philosophic acceptance of human weakness. Like Voltaire, he is interested in the way of the world and not the why of it. He does not propound
theories or pronounce judgment and criticizes only those who are incapable of conceiving of a possible relativity between good and evil, a basic
theme in Boulle's work.

Boulle blends literary influences, his own experiences, contemporary
events, and sound scientific ideas—with applications that border on the
outrageous—to create a unique body of work. "While adhering faithfully to the material facts," Boulle writes about the writer Cousin, the protagonist of *A Noble Profession,* "he had an inimitable talent for investing
them with some original significance that corresponded, without his
being aware of it, to his intuitive conviction, to his anxiety to satisfy
some higher authority or simply the requirements of his art" (Noble,
13). "My greatest pleasure in life," stated this brilliant storyteller, "is to
find a good idea for a novel."

Notes and References

Chapter One

1. Pierre Boulle, *L'île* (Paris: Editions de Fallois, 1991), 7; hereafter cited in text as *L'île*. Translations by Lucille F. Becker.
2. *My Own River Kwai,* trans. Xan Fielding (New York: Vanguard, 1967), 197; hereafter cited in text as *My Own.*
3. "The Duck Blind," in *Quia absurdum (sur la terre comme au ciel)* (*Because It is Absurd {on Earth as in Heaven}*), trans. Elizabeth Abbott (New York: Vanguard, 1970); hereafter cited in text as "Duck."
4. The episode of the duck blind is reminiscent of the conclusion of Flaubert's *Education sentimentale,* when the protagonist and his friend determine that the most memorable moment of their lives was one of nonconsummation.
5. *Mirrors of the Sun,* trans. Patricia Wolf (New York: Vanguard, 1983), 59; hereafter cited in text as *Mirrors.*
6. Interview with Lucille F. Becker, 19 November 1990; all such interviews hereafter cited in text.
7. *S.O.P.H.I.A.,* trans. Xan Fielding (New York: Vanguard, 1959), 15; hereafter cited in text as *S.O.P.H.I.A.*
8. *The Bridge over the River Kwai,* trans. Xan Fielding (New York: Vanguard, 1954), 167; hereafter cited in text as *Kwai.*
9. Boulle affirms that the episode of Loeken's bungalow is 95 percent exact. Interview with Lucille F. Becker, 12 April 1993.
10. A fixed-form poem derived from Malay poetry and consisting of a series of quatrains with alternate rhymes.
11. Pierre Boulle stated in an interview with Lucille F. Becker, 28 November 1992, that the principles employed by M. Bedoux were based on the "Bedeau" system, which really existed, and that is probably why he gave him a name that sounded so much like it. He added that he had perhaps overdone somewhat his caricature of M. Bedoux's relationship with the workers.
12. Boulle's demythologizing of the native beauties stands in amusing contrast to the romantic vision of the female bearers in the film version of *The Bridge on the River Kwai.*
13. His adventures with the trunk are described in detail in *S.O.P.H.I.A.* In an interview with Lucille F. Becker, 28 November 1992, Boulle stated that he met the director in his hotel room in London at the end of the war with the trunk still intact.
14. Ernest Hemingway, "Soldier's Home," in *The Short Stories of Ernest Hemingway* (New York: Charles Scribner's Sons, 1938), 147, 153.

15.   Boulle stated that his action was not prompted by Conrad's in an interview with Lucille F. Becker, 12 April 1993.

Chapter Two

1.   *Not the Glory,* trans. Xan Fielding (New York: Vanguard, 1955), 105–6; hereafter cited in text as *Glory.*

2.   The head of intelligence services is designated as X in the French novel but assumes the same identity as Sir Wallace in the English version. This change was made at the suggestion of the translator and approved by Pierre Boulle.

3.   *Face of a Hero,* trans. Xan Fielding (New York: Vanguard, 1956), 31–32; hereafter cited in text as *Hero.*

4.   Mireille is the name of the heroine of *Mireille* by Frédéric Mistral, the most famous author in the Provençal language and recipient of the Nobel Prize in 1904. The family of Boulle's mother, the Seguins, were publishers in Avignon who printed *Mireille.*

5.   François, duc de La Rochefoucauld, *Maxims* (Harmondsworth: Penguin, 1967), 51; hereafter cited in text.

6.   *A Noble Profession,* trans. Xan Fielding (New York: Vanguard, 1960), 9–10; hereafter cited in text as *Noble.*

7.   Maurice Shroder, "The Novel as a Genre," in *The Theory of the Novel,* ed. Philip Stevick (New York: Free Press, 1967), 25.

8.   *The Virtues of Hell,* trans. Patricia Wolf (New York: Vanguard, 1974), 57–58; hereafter cited in text as *Virtues.*

9.   The Burmese landscape and the trek described here were inspired by Boulle's journey as recounted in *My Own River Kwai.* The heavy bales of rubber produced on the plantations of Malaya, in which the heroin is hidden, also reflect Boulle's experiences as a rubber planter.

10.   R.-M. Albérès, *Le roman d'aujourd'hui 1960–1970* (Paris: Eds. Albin Michel, 1970), 33.

11.   *The Photographer,* trans. Xan Fielding (New York: Vanguard, 1968), 48–49; hereafter cited in text as *Photographer.*

12.   This title designates expertise in a field and could also be understood as "state of the art."

13.   When a B-movie actor became president of the United States, the cinematic aspects of life in Washington took on a surreal power. The trappings of statecraft, the facades and icons, began to resemble movie sets. The president really read his lines off cue cards; he really confused film memories with historical events. The great military fantasy of the era—Star Wars—took its name from a movie; it strongly resembled the doomsday device featured in a 1940 science-fiction film starring Ronald Reagan.

14.   *L'étrange croisade de l'empereur Frédéric II* (Paris: Flammarion, 1968), 13; hereafter cited in the text as *Frédéric.* Translations by Lucille F. Becker.

15.   See especially the story "Le poids d'un sonnet" (see chapter 4).

Chapter Three

1. Quoted by Georges Joyaux, "*The Bridge over the River Kwai:* From the Novel to the Movie," *Literature/Film Quarterly* 2 (1974): 179; hereafter cited in text.

2. Gilbert Ganne, "L'obsédé de la rivière Kwaï," *Nouvelles littéraires*, no. 2018 (5 May 1966): 11; hereafter cited in text. Translations by Lucille F. Becker.

3. Ian Watt, "The Myth of the River Kwai," *Observer* (September 1968): 18; hereafter cited in text as Watt 1968.

4. Ian Watt, "Bridges over the Kwai," *Partisan Review*, no. 26 (Winter 1959): 84; hereafter cited in text as Watt 1959.

5. An inversion of the number of Commando Force 136, where Boulle had trained in Calcutta.

6. Pierre Boulle, preface to *Le pont de la rivière Kwaï*, ed. G. J. Joyaux (New York: Scribners, 1963), xxi. Translation by Lucille F. Becker.

7. The last two lines of "If," a poem by Kipling in *The Days' Work.* Kipling's work glorified the Anglo-Saxon empire builders.

8. The film was financed by Columbia Pictures and directed by David Lean. The screenplay was written by two blacklisted American writers, Carl Foreman and Michael Wilson. When filming was complete, Sam Spiegel telephoned Boulle and said that two or three different writers had adapted the novel for the screen and that, since the screenplay adhered very closely to the novel, he was giving Boulle credit for the screenplay. Boulle agreed, not knowing the real reason, and received an Oscar for the screenplay. In an interview with Lucille F. Becker on 19 November 1990 Boulle said that when he later learned that the screenwriters were on a blacklist, he regretted having agreed. Had he known then the real reason, he would never have permitted his name to be used. Foreman and Wilson later claimed to have been cheated of both a credit and an Oscar. In 1985, both writers were posthumously awarded Oscars for the film.

9. Michael A. Anderegg, *David Lean* (Boston: Twayne Publishers, 1984), 94.

10. Watt, in "Bridges over the Kwai," 90, assures us from his firsthand experience that no prisoner on the railway ever succeeded in escaping.

11. The J. Peterman Company, "Owner's Manual," no. 23 (Summer 1993): 71.

12. Interview with Lucille F. Becker, 28 November 1992. Pierre Boulle does not know the ultimate fate of the Dutch girl.

13. *The Test,* trans. Xan Fielding (New York: Vanguard, 1957), 83; hereafter cited in text as *Test.*

14. *Webster's Unabridged Dictionary,* 13th ed., s.v. "amok": "A murderous frenzy that occurs chiefly among Malays, one that causes them to attack people at random."

15. *The Other Side of the Coin,* trans. Richard Howard (New York: Vanguard, 1958), 11; hereafter cited in text as *Coin.*

16. In a short story, "The Angelic Monsieur Edyh," Boulle transforms Stevenson's story of Doctor Jekyll and Mr. Hyde to show how unquestioning good can create destruction and havoc.

17. The "boy" is a 60-year-old Chinese man.

18. Gospel of Mark, 8:36.

19. *Ears of the Jungle,* trans. Michael Dobry and Linda Cole (New York: Vanguard, 1972), 14; hereafter cited in text as *Jungle.*

20. The struggle between human ingenuity and machines constitutes the story line of Boulle's short story "The Man Who Hated Machines," discussed in chapter 5.

Chapter Four

1. Steven Weinberg, *The First Three Minutes of the Universe* (New York: Basic Books, 1977), 155.

2. Pierre Boulle, *L'univers ondoyant* (The undulating universe) (Paris: Julliard, 1987), 7; hereafter cited in text as *Univers.* Translations by Lucille F. Becker.

3. To demonstrate that the theory of the universe that he propounds is held not only by science fiction novelists but also by the most brilliant scientists, Boulle quotes from *Cosmos,* by the noted astrophysicist Carl Sagan: "The laws of Nature are the same everywhere. The patterns in the spectra of distant stars and galaxies are the same as those for the Sun or for appropriate laboratory experiments: not only do the same chemical elements exist everywhere in the universe, but also the same laws of quantum mechanics that govern the absorption and emission of radiation by atoms apply everywhere as well. Distant galaxies revolving about one another follow the same laws of gravitational physics as govern the motion of an apple falling to the earth, or Voyageur on its way to the stars. The patterns of Nature are everywhere the same. Carl Sagan, *Cosmos* (New York: Random House, 1980), 296. Quoted in French by Boulle in *L'univers ondoyant,* 103.

4. Jill Milling, "The Ambiguous Animal; Evolution of the Beast-man in Scientific Creation Myths," diss., University of Texas at Dallas, 1985, 110–11.

5. *Garden on the Moon,* trans. Xan Fielding (New York: Vanguard, 1965), 8; hereafter cited in text as *Moon.*

6. Inexplicably named Stern in the English translation.

7. These brilliant men, working with one eye on the world of the future, were hounded by the very system they worked for. Von Braun was briefly arrested in 1944 by Himmler because he had been overheard saying that he was not really interested in weaponry but rather in space travel.

8. Stephen Kinzer, "Germans Plan, Then Cancel, Celebration of a Nazi Missile," *New York Times,* 29 September 1992, A1.

9. Quoted in David Halberstam, *The Fifties* (New York: Villard Books, 1993), 613.

10. Lucille F. Becker, "Science and Detective Fiction: Complementary Genres on the Margins of French Literature," *French Literature Series* 20 (1993): 122.

11. *Planet of the Apes,* trans. Xan Fielding (New York: Vanguard, 1963), 3; hereafter cited in text as *Planet.*

12. H. G. Wells, *The Island of Doctor Moreau* (New York: Duffield and Green, 1933), 216.

13. Surprisingly, the epilogue is deleted from the English translation.

14. *La planète des singes* (Paris: Julliard, 1963), 191.

15. All sequels and television series subsequent to the original film have no connection to Boulle.

16. Boulle expressed his approval of this change in an interview with Lucille F. Becker, 19 November 1990.

17. As in Shelley's poem "Ozymandias," "Round the decay / Of that colossal wreck, boundless and bare / The lone and level sands stretch far away."

18. This dénouement—a reminder of the final scene of H. G. Wells's *The Shape of Things to Come*—left one man and one woman alive to repopulate the world and, what is more, to star in an apparently endless series of brainless ape movies with not the slightest resemblance to Boulle's work. The *New York Times Magazine,* 9 January 1994, 13, reports that filmmaker Oliver Stone is planning a remake of *Planet of the Apes.*

19. Letter of Pierre Boulle to Lucille F. Becker, 7 February 1992.

20. *Desperate Games,* trans. Patricia Wolf (New York: Vanguard, 1973), 21; hereafter cited in text as *Games.*

21. A malady we have all witnessed pursuant to the plaintive cry: "The computers are down."

22. Aldous Huxley, *Ape and Essence* (New York: Harper & Brothers Publishers, 1948), 124.

23. Gilles Pudlowski, "Vous souvenez-vous de Pierre Boulle?" *Nouvelles littéraires* 59, no. 2775 (19–26 February 1981): 38.

24. Boulle refers the reader to an entry in the *Encyclopedia Britannica,* 15th ed., under the heading "psychical research," which is defined there as "the scientific study of such alleged occurrences as thought transference, foretelling the future, hauntings involving appearances of ghosts and movements of objects." While most scientists continue to reject the methods and findings of psychical or parapsychological phenomena, a growing number consider them an unproved possibility rather than an utter impossibility.

25. Brian Aldiss and David Wingrove, *Trillion Year Spree: The True History of Science Fiction* (London: Victor Gollancz, 1986), 8.

26. Pierre Boulle, *L'énergie du désespoir* (Paris: Julliard, 1981), flyleaf; hereafter cited in text as *Energie*. Translations by Lucille F. Becker.

27. Trouvères were poets of northern France in the Middle Ages.

28. *Le professeur Mortimer* (Paris: Fallois, 1987), 202. Translation by Lucille F. Becker.

29. *The Good Leviathan,* trans. Margaret Giovanelli (New York: Vanguard, 1978), 12–13; hereafter cited in text as *Leviathan.*

Chapter Five

1. *Contes de l'absurde* (Paris: Julliard, 1953) contains "Le poids d'un sonnet," translated by Lucille F. Becker (hereafter cited in text as "Poids") as well as four stories: "L'hallucination," "Une nuit interminable," "Le règne des sages," "Le parfait robot," which appear in *Time out of Mind, and Other Stories,* trans. Xan Fielding and Elisabeth Abbott (New York: Vanguard, 1966); stories from this collection are hereafter cited in text.

2. Pierre Versins, *Encyclopédie de l'utopie, des voyages extraordinaires et de la science-fiction* (Lausanne: L'Age de l'homme, 1972), 125.

3. The title of the anthology in English.

4. *Webster's Unabridged Dictionary,* 13th ed., s.v. "cybernetics": "the comparative study of the automatic control system formed by the nervous system and brain and by mechanoelectrical communications systems and devices," such as computing machines, thermostats, and photoelectric sorters.

5. Boulle describes the way in this problem was examined by the emperor Frederick II in *L'étrange croisade de l'empereur Frédéric II.*

6. Malcolm W. Browne, "Treading on Theologians' Ground, Physicist Wants to Weigh the Soul," *New York Times,* 4 January 1994, C9. All of the scientific instruments mentioned in the article do exist.

7. The four stories of the collection $E=mc^2$ (Paris: Julliard, 1957), "$E=mc^2$ ou le roman d'une idée," "L'amour et la pesanteur," "Les Luniens," and "Le miracle" appear in the English work *Time out of Mind, and Other Stories* and are hereafter cited in text.

8. This dedication appears in the revised French edition of $E=mc^2$, together with *Histoires charitables, Contes de l'absurde, Quia absurdum* (Paris: Julliard, 1992), 47.

9. William J. Broad, "Recipe for Love: A Boy, a Girl, a Spacecraft," *New York Times,* 11 February 1992, C1; hereafter cited in text.

10. All of the *Histoires charitables,* except for the "Histoire du bon petit écrivain" and "Le compte à rebours," appear in the English anthology *Time out of Mind, and Other Stories* and are hereafter cited in text. They included "L'arme diabolique," L'homme qui ramassait les épingles," "Le saint énigmatique," "L'homme qui haïssait les machines."

11. An amusing pastiche of Mark Twain.

12. *New York Times,* 31 August 1992, A2.

13.   See discussion of this story in chapter 1.

14.   *Because It Is Absurd (On Earth as in Heaven)* (New York: Vanguard, 1971), trans. Elisabeth Abbott, 37–38; hereafter cited in text. The stories in this collection are "Son dernier combat," "Le plombier," "Interférences," "L'affût au canard," "Quand le serpent échoua," "Les lieux saints," and "Le coeur et la galaxie."

15.   John Noble Wilford, "Ear to the Universe Is Plagued by Budget Cutters," *New York Times,* 7 October 1993, B12.

16.   "I borrow from *The Age of Robots* by Albert Ducrosq," Boulle writes, "the general principle of such a language; the principle only. I hope he will forgive me for no doubt having deformed it by diagramming it to extremes" ("The Heart and the Galaxy," 170).

17.   *The Marvelous Palace and Other Stories,* trans. Margaret Giovanelli (New York: Vanguard, 1977), 9; hereafter cited in text. The stories in this collection are "La grâce royale," "Le palais merveilleux," "Les limites de l'endurance," "Service compassion," "Les lois," and "L'angélique monsieur Edyh."

18.   Interview with Lucille F. Becker, 19 November 1990. "En religion, c'est le doute complet."

19.   No more grotesque than events transpiring around us. Tom Kuntz, "Beyond Singapore: Corporal Punishment, A to Z," *New York Times,* 26 June 1994, Section 4, 5. Kuntz, reporting from Bangladesh and citing an October 1993 report from Amnesty International, writes that several people have been sentenced to death by public stoning or burning or to public lashings in recent years by village councils, or *salish,* even though such sentences usurp Bangladeshi civil law. "A 14-year-old girl was sentenced by salish in August 1992 to 100 lashes after her rape by an influential villager," Amnesty International said. "The salish acquitted the rapist but took her pregnancy resulting from the rape as evidence of illicit sexual intercourse."

20.   Dr. J. Gayral, *Les délires de possession diabolique* (Paris: Vigot Frères, 1944).

21.   See chapter 3.

22.   *The Executioner,* trans. Xan Fielding (New York: Vanguard, 1961), 64; hereafter cited in the text as *Executioner.*

23.   See chapter 2.

24.   *Trouble in Paradise,* trans. Patricia Wolf (New York: Vanguard, 1985), 57; hereafter cited in text as *Paradise.*

25.   Larry B. Stammer, "Recasting the Virgin Mary in the Image of a Modern Day Woman: Changing an Ancient Religious Symbol to Suit Modern Fashions," *International Herald Tribune,* 2 February 1993, 1.

Chapter Six

1.   An idea Boulle expressed in the story "Histoire du bon petit écrivain."

2.   Letter of Pierre Boulle to Lucille F. Becker, 26 May 1992.

3.   *Le malheur des uns . . .* (Paris: Editions de Fallois, 1990), 11; hereafter cited in text as *Malheur.* Translations by Lucille F. Becker.

4. Boulle expressed this idea in the preface to the short story "The Marvelous Palace."

5. That is the fallacy in the film *The Bridge on the River Kwai,* where Nicholson sees the error of his ways. In Boulle's early novels, the protagonist is never confronted with reality.

6. *The Whale of the Victoria Cross,* trans. Patricia Wolf (New York: Vanguard, 1983), 10; hereafter cited in text as *Whale.*

7. Androclès, a Roman slave, is the hero of a story told by Aulu-Gelle. Thrown to the lions in the Roman circus, he was spared by a lion from whose paw he had once removed a thorn. The emperor pardoned him.

8. A romantic interlude inspired, according to Boulle, by personal experience, which he inserted into the novel. Interview with Lucille F. Becker, 19 November 1990.

9. Quoted by Gilles Pudlowski, "Vous souvenez-vous de Pierre Boulle?" *Nouvelles littéraires* 59, no. 2775 (19–26 February 1981): 38.

Selected Bibliography

Primary works are listed chronologically; secondary works are listed alphabetically; translations of primary works are listed alphabetically.

PRIMARY WORKS

Novels

William Conrad. Paris: Julliard, 1950.
Le sacrilège malais. Paris: Julliard, 1951.
Le pont de la rivière Kwaï. Paris: Julliard, 1952.
La face. Paris: Julliard, 1953.
L'épreuve des hommes blancs. Paris: Julliard, 1955.
Les voies de salut. Paris: Julliard, 1958.
Un métier de seigneur. Paris: Julliard, 1960.
La planète des singes. Paris: Julliard, 1963.
Le jardin de Kanashima. Paris: Julliard, 1964.
Le photographe. Paris: Julliard, 1967.
Les jeux de l'esprit. Paris: Julliard, 1971.
Les oreilles de jungle. Paris: Flammarion, 1972.
Les vertus de l'enfer. Paris: Flammarion, 1974.
Le bon Léviathan. Paris: Julliard, 1978.
L'énergie du désespoir. Paris: Julliard, 1981.
Miroitements. Paris: Flammarion, 1982.
La baleine des Malouines. Paris: Julliard, 1983.
Pour l'amour de l'art. Paris: Julliard, 1985.
Le professeur Mortimer. Paris: Editions de Fallois, 1987.
Le malheur des uns . . . . Paris: Editions de Fallois, 1990.

Philosophical tales

Le bourreau. Paris: Julliard, 1954.
Les coulisses du ciel. Paris: Julliard, 1979.
A nous deux, Satan! Paris: Julliard, 1992.

Short Stories

Contes de l'absurde. Paris: Julliard, 1953.
Contes de l'absurde, suivis de E=mc². Paris: Julliard, 1957.
Histoires charitables. Paris: Julliard, 1965.
Quia absurdum (sur la terre comme au ciel). Paris: Julliard, 1970.

139

Histoires perfides. Paris: Flammarion, 1976.

$E=mc^2$, *Histoires charitables, Contes de l'absurde, Quia absurdum (sur la terre comme au ciel).* Rev. ed. Paris: Julliard, 1992.

Autobiographical Works

Aux sources de la rivière Kwaï. Paris: Julliard, 1966.

L'îlon. Paris: Editions de Fallois, 1991.

Other

Walt Disney's Siam (screenplay). Lausanne: Nouvelles Editions, 1958.

William Conrad (play). Paris: Les Oeuvres Libres, 1962.

L'étrange croisade de l'empéreur Frédéric II (historical work). Paris: Flammarion, 1968.

L'univers ondoyant (essay). Paris: Julliard, 1987.

Works Translated into English

Because It Is Absurd (On Earth as in Heaven) (Quia absurdum {sur la terre comme au ciel}). New York: Vanguard, 1971.

The Bridge over the River Kwai (Le pont de la rivière Kwaï). New York: Vanguard, 1954.

Desperate Games (Les jeux de l'esprit). New York: Vanguard, 1973.

Ears of the Jungle (Les oreilles de jungle). New York: Vanguard, 1972.

The Executioner (Le bourreau). New York: Vanguard, 1961.

Face of a Hero (La face). New York: Vanguard, 1966.

Garden on the Moon (Le jardin de Kanashima). New York: Vanguard, 1965.

The Good Leviathan (Le bon Léviathan). New York: Vanguard, 1978.

The Marvelous Palace and Other Stories (Histoires perfides). New York: Vanguard, 1977.

Mirrors of the Sun (Miroitements). New York: Vanguard, 1986.

My Own River Kwai (Aux sources de la rivière Kwaï). New York: Vanguard, 1967.

A Noble Profession (Un métier de seigneur). New York: Vanguard, 1960.

Not the Glory (William Conrad). New York: Vanguard, 1955.

The Other Side of the Coin (Les voies de salut). New York: Vanguard, 1968.

The Photographer (Le photographe). New York: Vanguard, 1968.

Planet of the Apes (La planète des singes). New York: Vanguard, 1963.

S.O.P.H.I.A. (Le sacrilège malais). New York: Vanguard, 1959.

The Test (L'épreuve des hommes blancs). New York: Vanguard, 1957.

Time out of Mind, and Other Stories (Contes de l'absurde, $E=mc^2$, Histoires charitables). New York: Vanguard, 1966.

Trouble in Paradise (Les coulisses du ciel). New York: Vanguard, 1981.

The Virtues of Hell (Les vertus de l'enfer). New York: Vanguard, 1974.

The Whale of the Victoria Cross (La baleine des Malouines). New York: Vanguard, 1983.

SECONDARY WORKS

Books

Aldiss, Brian, and David Wingrove. *Trillion Year Spree: The True History of Science Fiction.* New York: Victor Gollancz, 1986. Comprehensive study of the science fiction genre.

Roy, Paulette. *Pierre Boulle et son oeuvre.* Paris: Julliard, 1970. Published doctoral thesis covering works published before 1968.

Articles

Allen, Louis. "To Be a Prisoner." *Journal of European Studies* 16, no. 64 (December 1986): 233–38. Finds *Le pont de la rivière Kwaï* successful in depicting the courage of resistance but a failure in its account of the nature of the enemy.

Anderegg, Michael A. "*The Bridge on the River Kwai* (1957)." In *David Lean,* 91–102. Twayne Filmmakers Series. Boston: Twayne Publishers, 1984. In this study of the work of director David Lean, the author discusses the making of the film based on Boulle's *The Bridge over the River Kwai.*

Battestini, Monique, and Gérard Klein, eds. *La grandiose avenir: Anthologie de la science-fiction française.* Paris: Seghers, 1975. Discussion and presentation of science fiction works published during the 1950s. Includes introduction to and text of Boulle's "Une nuit interminable."

Becker, Lucille F. "Science and Detective Fiction: Complementary Genres on the Margins of French Literature." *French Literature Series* 20 (1993): 119–25. Optimism of detective novel contrasted with pessimism of science fiction novel in George Simenon's *Maigret tend un piège* and Boulle's *La planète des singes.*

Ganne, Gilbert. "L'obsédé de la rivière Kwaï." *Nouvelles littéraires,* no. 2018 (5 May 1966): 1, 11. Interview with Boulle centering around *Aux sources de la rivière Kwaï.*

Gattégno, Jean. *La science-fiction.* Collection: Que sais-je? Paris: Presses Universitaires de France, 1983. Study of principal themes of science fiction. Boulle discussed pp. 71–72.

Jakubowski, Maxim. "French Science Fiction." In *Anatomy of Wonder: A Critical Guide to Science Fiction.* New York: Bowker, 1987.

Joyaux, Georges. "*The Bridge over the River Kwai:* From the Novel to the Movie." *Literature/Film Quarterly,* no. 2 (1974): 174–82. Discusses translation of the novel to film.

Knowlton, Edgar C. "Southeast Asia in the Works of Francis de Croisset and Pierre Boulle." *Proceedings of the 43rd Annual Symposium on Asian Studies* 3 (1982): 451–61. Southeast Asia in Boulle's works.

Milling, Jill. "The Ambiguous Animal; Evolution of the Beast-man in Scientific Creation Myths." Unpublished diss., University of Texas at Dallas, 1985. Study of beast-man includes discussion of the apes in *Planet of the Apes*.

Pudlowski, Gilles. "Vous souvenez-vous de Pierre Boulle?" *Nouvelles littéraires* 59, no. 2775 (19–26 February 1981): 38. Discusses *L'énergie du désespoir* and *Aux sources de la rivière Kwaï*.

Ross, Harris. *Film as Literature, Literature as Film*. New York: Greenwood Press, 1987. An introduction to and bibliography of the relationship of films to literature.

Suther, Judith D. "French Novelists and the American Phase of the War in Indochina." *Selecta: Journal of the Pacific Northwest Council on Foreign Languages,* no. 4 (1983): 1–9. Discusses several French novels on American involvement in Vietnam, including Boulle's *Les oreilles de jungle*.

Trousson, Raymond. *Voyages au pays de nulle part. Histoire littéraire de la pensée utopique*. Bruxelles: Editions de l'Université de Bruxelles, 1975. Study of utopian literature.

Versins, Pierre. *Encyclopédie de l'utopie, des voyages extraordinaires et de la science-fiction,* 125–26. Lausanne: L'Age de l'homme, 1972. Discusses "L'amour et la pesanteur" and "Une nuit interminable," two short stories which, according to Versins, guarantee Boulle immortality.

Viatte, A. L. "Le fantastique dans la littérature française." *La revue de l'université Laval* 19, no. 8 (April 1965): 715–20. Includes Boulle's *Contes de l'absurde* in discussion of the fantastic in French literature.

————. "L'oeuvre de Pierre Boulle." *La revue de l'université Laval* 8, no. 7 (March 1953): 617–21. Discusses biography, *William Conrad*, and *Le sacrilège malais*.

Watt, Ian. "Bridges over the Kwai." *Partisan Review* (Winter 1959): 83–94. Watt, a prisoner of war who worked on the Burma-Siam railway, analyzes Boulle's novel in the light of his own experiences.

————. "The Myth of the River Kwai." *Observer* (September 1968): 18–21, 23–26. Explains the way in which the film of Boulle's novel created a worldwide myth.

Index

The Author

Lucille Frackman Becker is a Drew University Professor Emerita of French. She received a B.A. from Barnard College, where she was elected to Phi Beta Kappa; a Diplôme d'Etudes Françaises from the University of Aix-Marseille, where she studied under a Fulbright grant; and an M.A. and Ph.D. from Columbia University. Her articles and reviews have appeared in numerous publications, among them *Montherlant vu par des jeunes de 17 à 27 ans, The Nation, Collier's Encyclopedia, Yale French Studies, Romanic Review, World Literature Today, Encyclopedia of World Literature in the 20th Century,* and *Contemporary World Writers.* Her books include *Henry de Montherlant* (Southern Illinois University Press, 1970), as well as *Louis Aragon* (1971), *Georges Simenon* (1977), *Françoise Mallet-Joris* (1985), and *Twentieth-Century French Women Novelists* (1989), which were published in Twayne's World Authors Series. Dr. Becker has lectured on modern French literature at universities in Thailand, Australia, New Zealand, Hong Kong, People's Republic of China, Sri Lanka, India, and Nepal. She was the keynote speaker at the National Press Club and at the International Monetary Fund during the 1987–88 Georges Simenon Festival in Washingon, D.C.

The Editor

David O'Connell is professor of foreign languages and chair of the Department of Foreign Languages at Georgia State University. He received his Ph.D. in 1966 from Princeton University, where he was a National Woodrow Wilson Fellow, the Bergen Fellow in Romance Languages, and a National Woodrow Wilson Dissertation Fellow. He is the author of *The Teachings of Saint Louis: A Critical Text* (1972), *Les Propos de Saint Louis* (1974), *Louis-Ferdinand Céline* (1976), *The Instructions of Saint Louis: A Critical Text* (1979), and *Michel de Saint Pierre: A Catholic Novelist at the Crossroads* (1990). He is the editor of *Catholic Writers in France since 1945* (1983) and has served as review editor (1977–79) and managing editor (1987–90) of the *French Review*.